Roux • Rick Stein • Richard Shepherd • Simon Fooks
no Borella • Benoît Blin • Albert Roux • Andrew Turner
dré Garrett • Adam Byatt • David Sh............en Purton
William Curley • Paul Askew • B............k Vadis
Doherty • Billy Campbell • David P............eathcote
liams • Claire Clarke • Gary Hunter • Luke Matthews
e Stanley • Frances Bissell • Gary Rhodes • Lawrence Keogh
Roux • Rick Stein • Richard Shepherd • Simon Fooks
no Borella • Benoît Blin • Albert Roux • Andrew Turner
dré Garrett • Adam Byatt • David Sharland • Ben Purton
William Curley • Paul Askew • Brian Turner • Nick Vadis
Doherty • Billy Campbell • David Pitchford • Paul Heathcote
liams • Claire Clarke • Gary Hunter • Luke Matthews
e Stanley • Frances Bissell • Gary Rhodes • Lawrence Keogh
Roux • Rick Stein • Richard Shepherd • Simon Fooks
no Borella • Benoît Blin • Albert Roux • Andrew Turner
dré Garrett • Adam Byatt • David Sharland • Ben Purton
William Curley • Paul Askew • Brian Turner • Nick Vadis
Doherty • Billy Campbell • David Pitchford • Paul Heathcote
liams • Claire Clarke • Gary Hunter • Luke Matthews
e Stanley • Frances Bissell • Gary Rhodes • Lawrence Keogh
Roux • Rick Stein • Richard Shepherd • Simon Fooks
no Borella • Benoît Blin • Albert Roux • Andrew Turner
dré Garrett • Adam Byatt • David Sharland • Ben Purton

Desert Island Dishes

*Recipes from the world's top chefs celebrating
130 years of Maldon sea salt*

Introduction by **Jay Rayner**

First published in 2012 by
Infinite Ideas Limited
36 St Giles
Oxford, OX1 3LD
United Kingdom
www.infideas.com

A CIP catalogue record for this book is available from the British Library

ISBN 978-1-908984-16-6

Brand and product names are trademarks or registered trademarks of their respective owners.

Food photographer Tony Briscoe
Food stylist Penny Stephens
Prop stylist Rebecca Williams

Project development and co-ordination by Richmond Towers Communications

Book designed and typeset at Cylinder

Printed in the UK by Butler Tanner and Dennis Ltd

Contents

Foreword

I love Sunday roast lunches, probably because of my upbringing. My father would always be in charge of carving the meat, and over the years it became a ritual. The meat would be left to rest and then my dad would carve the first slice and cut it into quarters. He would then taste one of the four pieces and give one to me. I would say, 'Dad that tastes great!' Dad would then sprinkle a little salt on top and say, 'Now try that.' The difference was phenomenal.

Now I take my dad's role in the ritual with my sons Simeon and Ben and grandchildren Lily Mae and Joe as the tasters. Of course I always use Maldon sea salt for its purity and enhancement of flavour and the kids all love it!

Maldon Salt Company has been an Associate Member of the Academy of Culinary Arts for nearly ten years and in that time has generously sponsored a number of Academy activities, including the Annual Awards of Excellence, the most prestigious award available to young people in the hospitality industry.

The Academy is Britain's leading professional association of Head Chefs, Pastry Chefs, Restaurant Managers and suppliers. It is committed to the education and training of young people in the hospitality industry through the provision of career opportunities, recognising and rewarding talent and raising standards and awareness of food, food provenance, cooking and service.

Our members are focused on mentoring and training the next generation of young people entering the industry.

The Academy's Associate Members are suppliers of the finest quality food and drink products. We are proud to have Maldon Salt Company as a Member; a testament to its quality is the number of Academicians who keep Maldon sea salt in their kitchens and cook with it every day.

Brian Turner CBE
President, Academy of Culinary Arts

Introduction

Like all obsessive cooks there are certain things I must always have close by when I'm at the stove: the wooden spoon with the burn marks on the handle from when I left it over the flame, the old metal tongs that spring just so in my hand. And then there's the simple white glossy cardboard box, which is always to the left of me and in easy reach. The typography on that box may have changed a little over the years but what's in it has not. The pyramid-shaped, snow-white crystals of Maldon salt, produced from the waters that lap the ancient Essex coastline, are a constant in my kitchen as in so many others in Britain and around the globe.

Maldon is just better than others. So much of the flavour of salt is in the shape of the crystals and the way they are experienced on the tongue. Fine ground table salt is a bare-knuckled and viciously blunt weapon. Maldon's flakes release their saltiness with a sweet precision, and add another layer of texture, of crunch. They are tactile. I adore taking a pinch of Maldon between the pads of thumb and middle finger and grinding them a little to break down the bigger crystals as I add them to a salad or to the outside of roast potatoes or, well, almost everything else besides.

But it's not just that. There's the knowledge that you are part of a community of cooks, for Maldon salt is one of the tightest links between the amateur and the professional kitchen. I have been a restaurant critic for over a dozen years, a life that has taken me inside countless restaurant kitchens, both grand and not so grand, and the one thing I can always be sure to find in there is a stock of Maldon salt. It is the salt others are measured by. If proof were needed take a look at the remarkable list of great cooks who have contributed to this book, published to celebrate the Maldon Salt Company's 130th birthday, with proceeds going towards the Academy of Culinary Arts.

There are recipes here from the likes of Albert Roux and Gary Rhodes, from Rick Stein, Brian Turner and many more besides. Plus Buckingham Palace seems to like the stuff too; Maldon has this year been awarded the Royal Warrant. The notion of a cookbook that puts salt in the spotlight may seem a little odd. After all isn't it one of those baseline ingredients that turns up in almost everything? Well yes, it is, but as the best cooks know, giving a damn about the basics is what distinguishes the merely ordinary chef from the good one.

To understand why Maldon is so special it's worth heading to the place it comes from on England's east coast, and the tiny business, with a staff of fewer than twenty, which continues to make it in the way it has always been made.

Today the company is in the hands of Steven Osborne, the fourth generation of the same family to have produced salt here since the works were first purchased in 1922 by his step great-grandfather, the serial entrepreneur James Rivers. However, the company has been trading as Maldon Salt Company on that site since 1882.

Once upon a time this area was heavy with salt works as the names of the local villages – Saltcote, Gore Saltings – attest. Many fell by the wayside, put out of business by punitive nineteenth-century salt taxes. Maldon, which takes its name from the nearby town, survived because back then it was also a coal merchants and had a diversified business. 'In those days the company was just an old shed down by the river,' Steven tells me. Today it has two sites and has grown from just three salt pans, the huge water baths from which the salt is crystallised, to nineteen, an expansion which was vital to keep up with demand.

Although they have swapped from coal-fired burners to gas, the salt-making method remains the same. The waters pulled from the Blackwater River are purified, boiled to 106°C to remove impurities and then heated for another sixteen or so hours until the salt crystallises out. It is 'drawn' by hand from the pan before being dried. For a while I watch Maldon employees Gary and Philip drawing the salt out of the pans, until it piles up like so many drifts of snow, at the water's edge. Between them these two men have been with the company almost half a century. It is a unique kind of continuity.

But none of this would be possible were it not for location. The Maldon salt we love so much is a function of geography, of geology and metrology. I stand on the salt marshes that edge the Blackwater River and look out at the cracked and fractured land. Rainfall is low here, meaning the saltiness of the water is not diluted by rain runoff further upstream. The tides rise a whacking six metres, swamping the land. When the waters draw back the salt crystallises out as the vegetation dries so that, when the tide next comes in, it picks up the extra salt. It's why the Maldon Salt Company takes water according to the lunar cycle, running production according to the push and pull of the moon. It's when it's saltiest.

In the old days, of course, their product was not necessarily regarded as anything particularly special. Steven Osborne has copies of adverts from the 1950s which recommend using '3/4lb to a full size bath'. You can throw a bucketload of Maldon in your bath if you like, but it does seem a bit of a waste. Wouldn't it find a better home helping to make David Simms' glorious homemade pork scratchings (page 21)? They come highly recommended. By me. Or to season the crust of Stefano Borella's rosemary focaccia (page 32)? Or as the title ingredient in Yolande Stanley's outrageous sounding Maldon sea salt nut caramel tart (page 173)? However you choose to use Maldon you'll be cooking with an important piece of culinary history. But more important even than that is the fact that you'll be cooking with something that will never let you down.

Enjoy.

Jay Rayner

Maldon Salt Company
– a pinch of history

The Maldon Salt Company has been producing salt in the UK for 130 years. Its history is long and rich and in the UK the Maldon Salt Company, now run by the fourth generation of the Osborne family, has become an institution. The key to its continued success lies in the production of a high-quality natural condiment that is made using traditional methods. Maldon salt is a prestigious and unique product known for its flavour and quality and sought after by the health-conscious and gourmets alike.

Maldon timeline

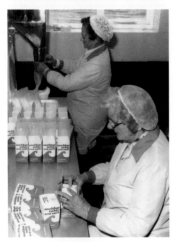

1882
Maldon Salt Company officially commences trading

1900
Maldon sea salt sold in Harrods and Fortnum & Mason

1922
Company bought by the Osborne family

1934
Cyril Osborne joins the business

1955
First export order to Sweden

1974
Clive Osborne joins the business

1977
Clive Osborne delivers a case of Maldon salt
to Buckingham Palace for the Queen's Silver Jubilee

1978
First order delivered to Sainsbury's supermarket

Maldon timeline

1981
The company moves over from coal to natural gas to heat salt pans

1984
Visit from Prime Minister Margaret Thatcher

1998
Steven Osborne joins the business

2000
Delia Smith recommends Maldon sea salt in her new cookbook

2001
Maldon Salt Company opens new offices, packaging and warehouse facility at Wycke Hill

2006
New production factory opens at Goldhanger

2010
Royal visit by Her Majesty The Queen

2012
Granted the Royal Warrant and 130th Birthday

The Essex salt makers

Salt has played an important role in our everyday lives for thousands of years, both flavouring and preserving our food.

For more than 2,000 years the east coast of Essex has played host to the age-old craft of harvesting salt using seawater. From the Iron Age through to Saxon times the estuaries and surrounding marshes were at the centre of the salt-making industry and the reddened earth and broken earthenware pots that form the Red Hills of Essex are evidence

of early salt production. These mounds of industrial waste are remnants of coarse pottery vessels, ash and scorched clay from fires used to heat the seawater.

It is thought that during high tide, seawater was trapped in clay pans cut into the river bank, where it was left to partially evaporate in the sun. The resulting brine was transferred into clay pots and heated over open fires. When evaporation was complete, the pots were broken open and the salt removed.

In 1086 the great Domesday survey recorded no fewer than forty-five salt pans in the Maldon area. For hundreds of years salt continued to be skilfully harvested using seawater but in the nineteenth century the Essex Salt Traders slowly disappeared and to this day, only a single company carrying out this age-old tradition has survived – Maldon.

Sea salt has been produced at Maldon for hundreds of years. The original salt works in Maldon, where Maldon salt is still produced, stands on a site that dates back to medieval times. Records go back to 1823, when Mr Robert Worraker, described as a 'saltmaker', occupied the building on the quayside. In 1882 the salt works was bought by Mr Thomas Elsey Bland and the Maldon Salt Company was born. The company was taken over in April 1922 by James and Nellie Rivers, the great-grandparents of the present owners, and decades later the Maldon Salt Company continues to grow and develop the age-old craft of harvesting salt using seawater.

The ancient craft of panning salt continues at Maldon today. The combination of low rainfall, strong winds and low-lying marshland produces good salty water. Seawater trapped in the marshes and on the vegetation evaporates to begin the process of crystallising the salt water naturally.

Seawater is evaporated in large stainless steel pans, using many of the old skills handed down by generations of salt-makers. The salt crystals are hand harvested daily using traditional long-handled rakes, a process known as 'drawing the pans'. The familiar pyramid-shaped crystals are characteristic of Maldon salt, which is recognised the world over as the finest salt available.

Sea salt is the growing choice of people who prefer a more natural flavour. Maldon salt is now one of the best loved and most widely recognised brands in the market. The soft, white, flaky crystals give Maldon salt a distinctive texture that sets it apart from other salts. Its clean fresh taste, milder than ordinary table salts, with no bitter aftertaste, is free from the chemical tang often associated with other salts and salt substitutes.

The popularity of sea salt in cooking has gained momentum significantly over the last decade, with support from celebrated chefs helping Maldon to maintain its place as the number-one producer of sea salt in the country. Maldon salt is just as famous overseas as it is on British shores and is exported and sold in more than forty-five countries worldwide, placing Essex and the town of Maldon firmly on the global map.

The Royal Warrant

Maldon Salt Company has recently been granted the prestigious Royal Warrant by Appointment to Her Majesty The Queen.

In fact Maldon has been supplying the Royal household's dinner table for decades – Clive Osborne even hand-delivered a box of Maldon sea salt to Buckingham Palace for the Queen's Silver Jubilee in 1977.

The company is one of approximately 850 businesses within British Trade and Industry to hold the accolade, entitling it to display the Royal Warrant on all products and literature.

Goujères (choux au fromage), page 16

Small bites

Lawrence Keogh

Head Chef, The Wolseley

Spiced glazed walnuts
with rosemary and Maldon sea salt

These are great warm, served as a bar snack or tossed through a salad, or served cold with cheese…

Ingredients

a drizzle of olive oil
20g butter
200g walnut halves
2 tsp brown sugar
1 tsp cayenne pepper
3 sprigs of rosemary, finely chopped
1 tsp Maldon sea salt
black pepper

Heat the olive oil and butter in a large pan over a medium heat. Add the walnut halves and the brown sugar, and toss them together for a few minutes, until caramelised. Stir in the cayenne pepper and rosemary, and season with Maldon salt and pepper. Stir everything together gently over a medium heat for a further 1–2 minutes, then tip into a bowl and serve.

Regis Negrier

Head Pastry Chef, The Delaunay

Goujères (choux au fromage)

In Burgundy, where I come from, goujères are served with Chablis or Kir. They are the most popular snack for a successful aperitif. My mother still takes time to make them whenever I visit her.

Ingredients

125ml water
125ml milk
125g butter
I tsp Maldon sea salt
250g plain flour
6 eggs, medium
10 turns of black pepper
   from a pepper grinder
a pinch of nutmeg
200g Emmenthaler cheese,
   cut into cubes no bigger than 0.5cm

Makes about 40 choux

Preheat the oven to 200°C/400°F/ gas 6. Bring the water, milk, butter and Maldon salt to the boil in a heavy-bottomed pan. Take the pan off the heat, add the flour and stir well. When the mixture is well combined, put the pan back on the heat and stir it with a spatula for a couple of minutes. Take the pan off the heat.

Let the mixture cool a little, and make a low well in the middle. Add the eggs, one at a time, stirring well until the paste becomes very smooth between each addition. At this point, if the dough is still warm, let it cool down until almost cold. Then add the black pepper, the pinch of nutmeg and the cheese cubes, and stir well to combine everything.

Using a teaspoon, portion the dough equally onto baking trays. Before baking, sprinkle some more Maldon salt on top of each goujère. Bake them until golden brown, which should take about 12–15 minutes.

Goujères (choux au fromage), page 16

Salted and spiced pumpkin seeds, page 21

David Simms

UK Executive Chef at Restaurant Associates / Roux Fine Dining

Pork scratchings

Trim the excess fat off the pork skin so that it is 0.5cm thick, then cut the skin into 1cm x 15cm lengths. Season the strips with the Maldon salt and paprika and leave to marinate for 2 hours. Wipe the excess marinade off the strips and dress with the oil.

Preheat the oven to 150°C/300°F/gas 2. Line a heavy or cast-iron baking sheet with silicone paper and arrange the strips in rows, ensuring you leave a gap in between each strip and around the edge. Place another sheet of silicone paper on top, followed by another baking sheet. Place in the oven and cook for 30 minutes.

Increase the oven temperature to 180°C/350°F/gas 4. Carefully remove the top tray and silicone paper and cook the pork for a further 15 minutes, or until the strips have puffed up and are golden brown. Remove them from the oven and drain on kitchen paper, and re-season with additional Maldon salt. Allow to cool, and serve.

Ingredients

500g rare breed pork skin
  (ideally from the belly)
1 tsp sweet smoked paprika
20g Maldon sea salt
50ml grapeseed oil

Ben Purton

Executive Head Chef, The Royal Horseguards Hotel and One Whitehall Place

Salted and spiced pumpkin seeds

Heat the oil in a frying pan until it is hot but not smoking. Be careful with the next part, as the seeds will spit at you a bit – add all the ingredients and toss them together until all the seeds are coated in the oil and well combined with the Maldon salt, pepper and chilli flakes. Cook them on a fairly high heat for 2–3 minutes and then drain them on kitchen paper.

If you can resist, they're ideal left to cool and served with a cold beer.

Ingredients

250g pumpkin seeds
2 tbsp good olive oil
1 tbsp Maldon sea salt
A couple of twists of freshly
  milled black pepper
A pinch of chilli flakes

Daniel Richardson

Head Chef, Hartwell House Hotel

Cod brandade

Cod brandade is very versatile. It can be used as a very tasty dip but I love to enjoy brandade with a little spinach, poached egg and hollandaise sauce, or with a refreshing salad in the summer for al fresco dining. It can also be personalised by adding garlic to the salting, or adding fresh micro-planed lemon zest when mixing the fish and potato – or, when serving, sprinkling it with some deep-fried crispy capers. These are just some ideas to play with…

Ingredients

500g cod fillet
100g Maldon sea salt
250ml milk
250ml water
a sprig of thyme
1 bay leaf
100ml olive oil
500g smooth mashed potato
  (made without adding any salt)

Serves 4, or 8 as a dip

The day before, sprinkle the cod fillet with the Maldon salt and put it in a dish. Cover the dish with cling film and leave it in the fridge overnight.

Put the milk, water, thyme and bay leaf in a medium pan. Bring to the boil and then remove from the heat. Leave to infuse for 10 minutes, then strain the liquid into a larger pan. Wash the cod fillet free from salt under running water, then put it into the herb-infused liquid. Cook it gently over a medium heat at just below a simmer – ideally 60–70°C – for 5 minutes. Allow the fish to cool in the liquid, and then carefully remove it from the pan. Finely flake the flesh from the skin, removing any bones.

Heat the olive oil in a clean pan over a low heat, then remove the pan from the heat and add the flaked cod. Mix the two together until the oil has been absorbed, then whisk in the mashed potato, and serve.

Simon Fooks

Head Chef, Merchant Taylors Catering

Gulls' eggs
with saffron Maldon sea salt flakes

Soak the gulls' eggs in warm water for a few minutes to stop them from cracking when they are cooked. Put a saucepan of salted water on to heat and bring to the boil. Add the gulls' eggs and cook for 6 minutes. Take the eggs out of the pan and refresh them in a bowl of iced cold water to prevent further cooking. When cooled, carefully remove half the shells evenly.

Soak a few stands of saffron in a couple of drops of water and then mix this into 70g of Maldon salt, which will dramatically change the colour. Place in a suitable salt dish.

Make a nest of watercress leaves on each serving plate, and arrange the eggs in it. Serve with the saffron salt and accompanied by brown bread and butter.

Ingredients

6 gulls' eggs
1 large bunch of watercress, washed and picked over
pinch of saffron
70g Maldon sea salt

Serves 2

Chilled English asparagus, page 46

To start...

Pretty much since humanity first clambered out of the trees and started wondering what was for dinner, salt has been our friend. It's not simply that it makes things taste nicer (though it does). It's that it is nature's best, most natural and reliable preservative, and we need those to help us get through the cold, lean months. There are few culinary traditions around the world in which curing with salt to lengthen the lifespan of perishable foodstuffs does not feature in one way or another, from the salt beefs and porks of Eastern Europe and the US through the cured fish of Scandinavia and the hams of Spain and Italy to the pickles of Korea and Japan. And unsurprisingly it features very heavily in this selection of starters.

For salt-curing doesn't just make things last longer. As moisture is drawn out it deepens and intensifies flavour and adds an extra dimension to the texture. It makes them denser and less flabby. Try Robert Kirby's Maldon cured salmon with beetroot and dill or Steven Doherty's gravadlax or Luke Matthews' wasabi marinated salmon, each of them giving their own spin on the same principle. As Paul Gayler proves with his salt-grilled chermoula mackerel, it's also a brilliant friend to the richer, oilier fish, and in Terry Tinton's scallop dish and Richard Shepherd's prawn salad, it does marvellous things to bring out the natural sweetness of the best of seafood. Here then is a selection of smaller dishes – from gutsy Mediterranean soups, through robust salads to terrific things to do with asparagus – all designed to waken the palate up and build the appetite. But you wouldn't be blamed for wanting to make any of them the main event. In which case just double up the quantities. Nobody will tell you off.

Jay Rayner

Paul Askew

Food and Beverage Director and Chef Patron, The London Carriage Works and Hope Street Hotel

King scallop with braised pork cheek and morcilla,
served with cauliflower purée, golden raisin dressing and jus

Ingredients

4 large king scallops in shells, cleaned
4 slices morcilla (Spanish black pudding)
A little butter

For the pork cheeks:
4 pork cheeks
25g butter
1 tsp oil
1 carrot, peeled and diced
1 stick celery, peeled and diced
1 medium onion, peeled and diced
100ml organic cider
5 sprigs of thyme
300ml brown stock

For the cauliflower purée:
1 waxy new potato, such as Sputna (Cyprus new potatoes)
1 small cauliflower, trimmed and chopped
100g butter
6 garlic cloves, peeled
50ml double cream
Maldon sea salt
pepper

For the dressing:
a little vegetable oil
50g golden raisins
1 large shallot, peeled and diced
100ml Chardonnay vinegar
100ml fino sherry

For the salad:
1 frisee lettuce
a handful of sorrel
1 Granny Smith apple
a little white wine vinegar and olive oil
a little meat jus

Serves 4

Start with the pork cheek. Preheat the oven to 160°C/320°F/gas 2–3. Trim all the outside sinew off the cheek, leaving a clean piece of meat. Season the meat. In a hot pan seal the meat until golden brown all over. Put the vegetables, cider, stock and herbs into an ovenproof casserole. Add the pork cheeks and cook for 4 hours until tender. Strain the cooking liquor and reduce it down until it has the consistency of a jus. If you have the appropriate equipment, vacuum pack the cheeks individually with a little sauce, and reheat them in a water bath to serve. Otherwise, keep both the cheeks and the sauce warm.

To make the cauliflower purée, cook the potato, cauliflower and three cloves of garlic in salted water with the butter until soft, which will take about 20 minutes. Drain thoroughly, retaining a little of the cooking liquor, and then liquidise them carefully while still hot. Add a little liquor if necessary, and a splash of cream and seasoning and blend until smooth.

Make the dressing next. Warm the golden raisins and diced shallot in a pan with a splash of oil and seasoning. Add a little Chardonnay vinegar and fino sherry and reduce the liquid by half. Leave the dressing to cool but warm it a little before serving. Just before you are ready, make the salad. Cut the apple into julienne strips and add some lettuce leaves and sorrel. At the last minute, dress these with olive oil and vinegar.

Now to assemble the dish. Warm the purée and the pork cheeks if necessary. Put some oil into a thick-bottomed sauté pan, and heat it up ready for the scallops. Place the scallops in the pan along with a sprinkling of Maldon salt. Allow to caramelise until golden brown before turning – this will only take a minute – then flip them over and cook the other side. Then add the morcilla and a knob of butter and cook for another minute or so.

To serve, put a spoonful or two of purée on each plate. Then place the scallop, morcilla and pork cheek on the purée in a line for neatness of presentation. Add the salad and a tablespoon of dressing, followed by a little jus to finish.

Tip: This is a beautiful, complex dish and one of my favourites, with six main elements and a little salad to garnish… enjoy!

Frances Bissell

Consultant Chef and Food Writer

Fragrant tea-smoked salmon

I learned this method for tea-smoking from its originator, Bruce Coste, years ago in San Francisco. Smoking your own fish is not nearly as complicated as you might think – and you do not need a special smoker, you can improvise with what you have in the kitchen. I once had a rack made out of chicken wire, and I have also used the foil trays from ready-made pies, cutting out sufficient foil to let the smoke swirl around the fish.

Crush the Maldon salt and the two peppers in a mortar then toast them lightly in a dry wok. When they are cool, rub the mixture all over the fish.

Carefully line the wok with a double thickness of foil. Put the rice, sugar and tea in the bottom. Then place the rack on top, grease it lightly and arrange the fish fillets on it. Put more foil around the edge of the wok and put the lid on, then pull the foil up to create a seal around the lid (you can also use damp paper towels, rolled up).

Place the wok on a medium to high heat, and once the rice and sugar have begun to smoke – which you will smell rather than see, resist the temptation to open the lid – leave it for 10–15 minutes. Then remove it from the heat and, still with the lid firmly on, leave for a further 15 minutes.

The smoked salmon can be served, quite simply, as a starter. As a main course, serve the fish warm with mashed potatoes into which you have stirred plenty of chives, with a lemon butter sauce. It is also good cold, with a salad. And leftovers make very fine fish cakes...

Ingredients

6 x 175g pieces salmon fillet
1 tbsp Maldon sea salt
1 tbsp Szechuan pepper
1 tbsp black peppercorns
100g uncooked rice
100g sugar
A handful of Lapsang Souchong, Oolong, Earl Grey or other distinctive tea leaves

Serves 6

Stefano Borella

Group Pastry Chef / Lecturer at La Cucina Caldesi Cookery School, Caldesi Restaurants Ltd

Focaccia al rosmarino
– rosemary focaccia

I was taught how to make focaccia by a Tuscan baker. He told me to tuck the flavourings into bed and pull the duvet over them! He explained that if you leave sprigs of rosemary sticking up they burn and do not offer any flavour to the bread, so push them in and partially cover them in dough.

Ingredients

500g strong white bread flour
2 tsp Maldon sea salt
15g fresh yeast or dried equivalent
  (usually half the amount of fresh;
  follow packet instructions)
300ml tepid water
90–100ml extra virgin olive oil
a little plain white flour, for dusting
Maldon sea salt,
  for sprinkling prior to baking
1 large sprig of rosemary

Other topping ideas:
Thyme, olives, red onion slices

Serves 8–10

Mix the flour and Maldon salt together in a large mixing bowl. Blend the yeast into the tepid water with your fingers until no lumps remain. Add the yeast liquid and 2½ tablespoons of the oil to the flour and mix well, using a plastic scraper or your hand. When the liquid is incorporated, bring all the ingredients together into a ball of dough with your hand. Use the dough to pick up the bits from the sides of the bowl so that you leave the bowl clean.

Turn the dough out onto a lightly floured work surface and knead it by pulling, stretching and folding for around 10 minutes. The dough should be soft, but if it is really sticky add a little more flour. When the dough is worked enough it should bounce back to the touch and feel elastic; if it doesn't, keep kneading.

Fold the edges of the dough underneath so that you have a smooth rounded ball. The top will be the surface of your focaccia. Grease the bowl with 20ml of the olive oil to prevent the dough sticking to it. Put the smooth top side of the dough head first into the oiled bowl, and turn it over to coat the top and sides with oil (this will prevent a crust forming and stop it sticking). Cover the bowl with cling film or place a tea towel over it and leave it in a warm, draught-free spot for about an hour, or until the dough has doubled in volume.

Continued on page 34…

Stefano Borella

Group Pastry Chef / Lecturer at La Cucina Caldesi Cookery School, Caldesi Restaurants Ltd

Focaccia al rosmarino *Continued*

Next, slide the dough onto an oiled baking sheet or roasting tin. Gently ease it out of the bowl from underneath, trying to keep a good rounded edge. Then use your fingertips to make indentations in the dough, flattening it into an oval or circle about 3 centimetres thick. Add your choice of toppings and drizzle over 30ml of oil – but no Maldon salt yet. Break sprigs of rosemary (or thyme) off the main stem and tuck into the dough; press olives and onion rings into the dough to stop them burning.

Return the dough to rise in its warm, draught-free place until it is about half as high again – this will take 30–40 minutes.

Preheat the oven to 220°C/425°F/gas 7. When the dough has risen, use your fingertips again, gently, to press more indentations into the dough. Drizzle with the remaining olive oil and sprinkle with Maldon salt. Bake in the oven for about 15–20 minutes or until golden brown. If the bottom is not cooked – it should sound hollow when tapped – turn the focaccia over and bake it for a further 5 minutes.

Remove it from the oven and allow it to cool on a wire rack so that it cannot sweat underneath.

Tip: Focaccia doesn't keep well but if you want to eat it the next day, allow it to cool then wrap it in cling film to stop it drying out. To use up any left-over focaccia, split in half, cut into large soldiers and toast. Top with squashed oven-dried tomatoes or sun-dried tomato, caper and olive paste…

Luke Matthews
Executive Chef, Chewton Glen

Herb-rolled yellow fin tuna
with wasabi, mango and coriander

Preparing the tuna can be done a day in advance. Take the tuna loin, cut it in half lengthways, then round the edges off with a knife to form a barrel shape. Season with Maldon salt and pepper, then sear it in a hot frying pan until coloured on all sides. Remove it from the pan and allow it to cool. Then brush it all over with Dijon mustard (this acts like a glue) and roll it in the chopped herbs. Wrap it very tightly in cling film and put it in the fridge.

The pickled vegetables and ginger also need to be made in advance. For the vegetables' pickling liquid, mix together the water, vinegar, oils, lime juice and sugar in a large pan. Wrap the coriander, garlic and lemon grass in muslin, then add to the rest of the pickling mixture. Bring the pan up to a simmer and then drop in the carrot and fennel, and cook till they are al dente. Then add the pepper and onion, remove the pan from the heat and allow the liquid to infuse and cool (the beansprouts are combined with the pickled vegetables when you assemble the dish).

Wash the ginger and rub the skin off. Slice the peeled ginger thinly, and then salt the slices. Leave them in a bowl for 1 hour. Dry the slices with kitchen paper and put them in a large sterilised jar. Mix the rice vinegar and sugar and bring to the boil, then pour the hot mixture over the ginger and allow to cool. Cover the jar and refrigerate – and note that pickled ginger may change colour to light pink.

The rest of the dish can be done before serving. Prepare the liquid for the pickled mooli. Put the rice wine vinegar, sugar, chilli and coriander seeds in a pan. Bring to the boil, then take the pan off the heat and leave the mixture to cool down and infuse.

Continued on page 37…

Ingredients

For the herb-rolled tuna:
1kg centre-cut tuna loin
Maldon sea salt and black pepper, to season
20g parsley, chopped
20g tarragon, chopped
20g chervil, chopped
enough Dijon mustard to coat the loin

For the pickled vegetables:
500ml water
150ml Chardonnay wine vinegar
50ml olive oil
30ml sesame oil
juice of 1 lime
1 tbsp sugar
3 lemon grass stalks, chopped
1 clove of garlic, crushed
1 tbsp coriander seeds
1 carrot, peeled and sliced
1 bulb of fennel, cut in batons
1 red pepper, cut in batons
1 yellow pepper, cut in batons
1 medium red onion, sliced
50g beansprouts

For the pickled ginger:
500g fresh ginger
1 tsp Maldon sea salt
330ml rice vinegar
200g sugar

Luke Matthews

Executive Chef, Chewton Glen

Herb-rolled yellow fin tuna *Continued*

Make the wasabi dressing next. Put the wasabi paste, lime zest and juice, rice wine vinegar, honey and Maldon salt in a liquidiser. Blend, and slowly add the oils. Transfer to a squeeze bottle, if possible.

Now assemble the dish. Peel the mooli, cut it in half lengthways and slice as thinly as possible. Toss the mooli in its pickling liquid. Lie a piece of the mooli in the centre of the plate. Drain the pickled vegetables and arrange some, mixed with a few beansprouts, on the mooli with a few slices of the pickled ginger. Unwrap the tuna and slice it finely, then arrange it on top. Using the squeeze bottle, pull a line of the wasabi dressing either side of the fish (in the absence of a squeeze bottle, use a small jug and pour as fine a line as possible). Lie some diced mango and herbs on, and top with a few Maldon salt flakes.

For the pickled mooli:
400ml rice wine vinegar
a scant tsp sugar
half a red chilli
½ tbsp coriander seeds
a small piece of mooli (about 100g)

For the wasabi dressing:
1 x 50g tube of wasabi paste
zest and juice of 1 lime
25ml rice wine vinegar
25g clear honey
Maldon sea salt, to taste
200ml groundnut oil
100ml olive oil

To garnish:
1 mango, diced
some micro coriander
red amaranth (if possible)
Maldon sea salt

Serves 10

Adam Byatt

Chef Proprietor, Trinity Restaurant

Beetroot-cured salmon gravadlax

Ingredients

1 x 1kg filleted side of salmon
250g caster sugar
250g Maldon sea salt
250g raw beetroot
1 large orange
10g lemon verbena tea leaves
half a bunch of dill

To serve:
sourdough bread
caper berries
pickled beetroot

Serves 8

Weigh the salmon accurately, to check that you have the right quantity of sugar and Maldon salt for the cure. The sugar and salt combined in equal quantities should be half the weight of your fish.

Remove the pin bones from the salmon and score the skin in four places to allow the cure to be absorbed. Wash, peel and roughly chop the beetroot. Peel the zest from the orange and reserve it, then halve the fruit and squeeze the juice.

Put the sugar and Maldon salt into a food processor. Add the beetroot, tea leaves and dill with the orange zest and juice, and blend to a fine pulp. Lay the salmon skin-side down in a shallow ceramic dish and cover it completely with the cure mixture. Cover the dish with cling film and leave the salmon to cure for 4 days in the fridge, turning the fish and basting it with the cure mixture after 2 days.

When the curing time is up, scrape the cure off the salmon and lift the fish out of the dish. Rinse the remaining cure away under cold running water, then pat the fish dry with a cloth – the flesh will be bright red and firm to the touch.

Starting at the wider end of the salmon, slice it thinly with a sharp knife angled slightly towards the opposite end of the fish, stopping just before you get to the skin. You should have about six slices per person. Lay these slices on a plate and accompany them with sourdough bread – and pots of goodies like caper berries and pickled beetroot.

Tip: If beetroot isn't your thing, simply omit it and add whatever takes your fancy, as long as the flavours are pronounced. A few of my favourite ingredients are star anise, grapefruit and basil. Treat the grapefruit like the orange in the recipe, and blend it to a pulp in the food processor with the star anise, a handful of basil leaves, the sugar and Maldon salt. The blend will not be eaten, so chunky pieces are fine.

Billy Campbell

Executive Chef, Thistle Glasgow

Slow-cooked tomato and basil soup

Cut the tomatoes in half and halve the cloves of garlic. Put them in a bowl with half the fresh basil, thyme, balsamic vinegar, olive oil, sliced shallots and some seasoning. Mix everything together, cover the bowl and put it in the fridge to marinate for 24 hours.

The next day, preheat the oven to 150°C/300°F/gas 2. Transfer the marinated tomatoes and shallots into a roasting tin or earthenware dish and cook them slowly for 2–3 hours.

Warm a large heavy-bottomed saucepan over a moderate heat. Add the butter and allow it to melt, then add the sliced white onions and cook them slowly until they are soft but have not begun to colour. Now add the tomato purée and cook it out for 2–3 minutes. Then add the slow-cooked tomatoes to the pan of softened onions. Mix them together well and add the stock, then simmer for a further 20 minutes.

Take the pan off the heat. Add the rest of the basil, stir it in and then liquidise the soup in a blender. Serve the soup in warmed bowls.

Ingredients

900g plum tomatoes
3 large cloves of garlic
50g basil leaves
6 sprigs of fresh thyme
150ml balsamic vinegar
150ml olive oil
  (preferably Frutatto Virgin Olive Oil)
225g shallots, peeled and sliced
50g butter
225g white onions, peeled and sliced
3 tbsp tomato purée
1.25 litres vegetable or chicken stock
Maldon sea salt and milled black
  pepper, to taste

Serves 4

Jim Cowie

Chef Patron, Captain's Galley Seafood Restaurant

Sorrel-infused mackerel fillets

Ingredients

6 mackerel fillets (skin removed)
150g Maldon sea salt
1.75 litres still mineral water
a good bunch of sorrel leaves
500ml 'low flavour' oil
  – vegetable, groundnut, etc
1 large white onion, thinly sliced
  into rings

Serves 3–6, depending on how you
use the fillets!

Sprinkle most of the Maldon salt evenly over a board. Place the mackerel fillets on top of the salt, skin side down, then sprinkle a teaspoon of Maldon salt over each fillet. Place the board at a slant to allow the juices to drain away from the fish, and leave overnight.

At the same time fill a saucepan with the mineral water and bring it to the boil. Add twelve sorrel leaves, then set it aside to cool completely. Transfer it to a bowl and put it in the fridge overnight.

Next day, wipe off any excess salt and moisture left on the fish. Add the fish to the sorrel and water mix, and leave them to infuse for 6 hours.

Warm the crock pot or slow cooker up to a good room temperature. In a separate saucepan, heat the oil to 60°C, add the sliced onion rings and cook until they lose their opaque appearance and become translucent. Transfer the mackerel fillets to the crock pot and then pour the oil and onion mix into the pot on top of the mackerel, making sure the fillets are completely covered in the oil. Close the pot. When it has cooled down, set it in the fridge and leave for a further 24 hours (you may need to transfer the contents to another container; if so, make sure the fish is completely covered). Then take the fish out as required, and use in salads, canapés, etc.

Stephen Doherty

Chef Director, First Floor Café, Lakeland Ltd

Home-cured gravadlax
with a sweet-grain mustard relish

Prepare the salmon. Coarsely grind the peppercorns, then mix them together with half the dill, and all the sugar and Maldon salt. Put the salmon in a deep tray and cover both sides with the salt mixture. Cover the tray and leave it in the fridge or a cold place for 24 hours.

The next day, remove the salmon from the salt mixture and rinse it under cold running water. Dry the salmon on a wire tray in a cold place for 48 hours.

Put the salmon on a piece of greaseproof paper and coat both sides with the Dijon mustard and the remainder of the dried dill. Shake off any excess dill (you can keep it to use another time, if you wish). Then put the salmon in a cold place to cure for another 24 hours. Finally, slice it thinly and serve – or wrap it in cling film and refrigerate; it will keep well for 2 weeks.

Serve it with a mustard relish. Mix all the relish ingredients together well, then transfer the mixed relish to an airtight container and refrigerate – it will keep for a month.

Ingredients

For the salmon:
1 x 2kg fully trimmed, skin on, side of salmon – boned
50g whole white peppercorns
50g dried dill weed
50g caster sugar
1kg Maldon sea salt
2 tbsp Dijon mustard

For the relish:
100g Dijon mustard
100g wholegrain mustard
65g caster sugar
2 tsp dried dill weed
a splash of white wine vinegar, to taste
a dribble of sunflower oil – enough to get the right consistency

Serves 10–12

Chris and Jeff Galvin

Chef Patrons, Galvin Restaurants

Chilled English asparagus
with truffle vinaigrette

Ingredients

40 large spears of English asparagus
75ml truffle juice (if truffle juice
    is unavailable see alternative
    suggestion below)
1 tbsp brown chicken jus
1 tsp sherry vinegar
a pinch of table salt
200ml groundnut oil
50ml black truffle oil
1 tbsp extra virgin olive oil
12 shavings of black truffle
4 sprigs of chervil
Maldon sea salt

Serves 4

Trim the asparagus by snapping off the base of the stems, then peel the spears from just below the tip. Blanch them in a large pan of boiling salted water for 3–4 minutes, then drain. Refresh in iced water until completely cold, then drain again and spread them out on a clean cloth. When they are dry, put them in the fridge.

For the vinaigrette, boil the truffle juice, chicken jus and vinegar together until reduced by half. Transfer the resulting liquid to a mixing bowl and allow it to cool. Add a small pinch of table salt and then, using an electric hand whisk on its slowest speed, add just a few drops of groundnut oil. Continue adding it very gradually, just a few drops at a time; the mixture should come together and start to thicken. This will take time; don't be tempted into adding more than about half a teaspoonful at once. When all the groundnut oil has been incorporated, add the truffle oil in the same manner. Finally, adjust the seasoning and the consistency, adding a little water if the vinaigrette is too thick; it should be thick enough just to hold its shape.

Cut the asparagus into spears 14cm long, put them in a mixing bowl and toss with the olive oil, using just enough to coat them.

To serve, lie the asparagus spears neatly on serving plates, place the truffle shavings on top and, using two tablespoons, place a quenelle of the thick vinaigrette to the side. Garnish with the chervil sprigs and a pinch of Maldon salt.

An alternative to truffle juice…
Substitute a rich mushroom stock. Roast 400g of roughly chopped mushrooms – stems and all – in a medium-hot oven until lightly browned. Put them in a large pan and add water to cover; about 500ml. Bring to the boil and simmer for 1 hour. Then strain the mushrooms over a bowl, pressing them into the sieve to extract the maximum amount of juice. Return the liquid to the pan and put it back on the heat. Boil it until it reduces by half, and pass it through a fine sieve or chinois before use.

André Garrett, MCA
Head Chef, Galvin at Windows

Warm salad of salt-baked heritage beetroots and carrots
with whipped goat's curd and a walnut and date purée

Preheat the oven to 200°C/400°F/gas 6. Wash, gently scrub and clean all the vegetables with a small knife; do not peel them.

Mix all the salt crust ingredients together in a large bowl to form a paste or soft dough. Roll this paste out on a floured surface. Then wrap each vegetable up in some of the paste; push the edges together to seal it. Lay the wrapped vegetables on a baking tray, and bake for 45 minutes–1 hour until they are cooked. Take them out and set them aside to cool.

Make the walnut and date purée while the vegetables are cooking. Toast the walnuts in a dry frying pan over a medium heat and set them to one side. Crush all the spices in a pestle and mortar and toast them in the warm dry pan for a couple of minutes too. When the scent begins to rise, pour on the balsamic vinegar and heat it through. Add the sugar and the orange peel and allow them to infuse for a few minutes. Put the dates and walnuts in a bowl, then pass the orange-infused vinegar through a sieve onto them – reserve the orange peel. Transfer the date and walnut mixture to a blender and blend to a fine purée. Chop the reserved orange peel very finely and stir it through the date purée. Set it aside at room temperature.

When the vegetable parcels are cool to the touch, break the crusts open and remove the vegetables; they should be cooked but still firm to your touch. Scrape off the skins carefully. Cut the vegetables into various slices and shapes to present nicely on the plate; try to keep them small and elegant. Set them aside.

Whip all the goat's curd ingredients together in a large bowl until they are smooth. Carefully transfer them to a piping bag with a 1cm plain nozzle, put the bag in a dish and chill it in the fridge.

Now take the cut vegetables and warm them very gently in a low oven; warm the serving plates too. Put the vegetables into a bowl and dress them with a few drops of olive oil and a few pinches of Maldon salt. Using a small palette knife, spread a little date purée across each plate and dress the vegetables elegantly across the purée. Pipe small domes of goat's curd around the salad – we allow five per plate – drop a few rocket leaves over it, and drizzle with a little more olive oil. Serve immediately.

Ingredients

2 yellow heritage beetroots, tennis ball size
2 red heritage beetroots, tennis ball size
2 yellow heritage carrots
2 red heritage carrots

For the salt crust:
500g plain flour
400g water
200g Maldon sea salt
2 sprigs of thyme
5 twists of a black pepper mill

For the walnut and date purée:
40g shelled and chopped walnuts
1 small piece of cinnamon stick
1 clove
5 black peppercorns
2 juniper berries
100ml white balsamic vinegar
60g fresh dates, peeled, pitted and chopped
1 tsp sugar
1 strip of orange peel

For the whipped goat's curd:
100g fresh goat's curd
4 tsp double cream
1 tsp Champagne vinegar
white pepper, 2 twists of a mill

To serve:
A little good olive oil to dress the salad
A few pinches of Maldon sea salt
20 small rocket leaves

Serves 4

Paul Gayler

Executive Chef, The Lanesborough

Duck prosciutto

This is my recipe for salt-cured duck breast, prepared like prosciutto (Parma ham); it is simple to prepare and fairly inexpensive to make. For the best results the meat should be thinly sliced on a gravity food slicer, but thinly sliced with a knife is fine.

Ingredients

2 x 225g duck breast
100g Maldon sea salt
50g caster sugar
2 bay leaves, shredded
1 tbsp fresh thyme leaves
½ tbsp chopped rosemary
1 tbsp cracked black peppercorns

Serves 4 as a starter

Using a sharp knife, remove most of the skin from the duck, leaving just a thin layer of fat on the breast. In a bowl, mix together all the remaining ingredients.

Place half the Maldon salt mix in a shallow dish, then put the duck breasts on top, fat side down. Cover them with the remaining mixture, ensuring the breasts are totally immersed in the salt mix. If there isn't enough to cover them completely, add more salt. Cover the dish with cling film. Put it in the fridge for 36 hours – and note that any longer will shrink the duck breasts in size and render them tough.

Remove the breasts from the salt, rinse them under a little cold running water, then dry them well on a cloth. Put them in the freezer for 2 hours, which makes them easier to slice.

Slice them thinly, ready to serve, and ensure they are defrosted before serving.

Tip: I like this duck strewn over a crisp leaf salad with thinly sliced pear, crumbled blue cheese, red wine vinaigrette… absolutely delicious.

Paul Gayler

Executive Chef, The Lanesborough

Salt-grilled chermoula mackerel

Chermoula is a marinade or sauce from Morocco or Tunisia; it is wonderfully fragrant and with a hint of spiciness. Here the fish is first marinated and then cooked under a hot grill; the thin film of Maldon salt which coats the fish keeps it beautifully moist as it cooks. I like to serve this dish with some buttered spinach tossed with pine nuts and raisins, couscous and a spoonful of my chopped preserved lemons (see page 76).

Line a large grilling tray with a sheet of buttered kitchen foil. Rinse the mackerel under a little cold running water, and then dry them in a cloth. Using a small sharp knife, make slits on either side of the fish down to the bone; this will allow the flavour to get right into the fish while it marinates. Place the lemon slices in the cavity of the fish, then put the fish on the grilling tray.

In a bowl, mix the ginger, garlic, lemon juice, coriander and spices to form the marinade. Using a brush – or your hands – spread the marinade all over both sides of the fish, ensuring it gets right down to the central bone. Set aside for 30 minutes at room temperature before cooking.

When you are ready to cook the mackerel, sprinkle both sides of the fish with the Maldon salt, but give the tail area a thicker coating as this will help to prevent burning.

Preheat the grill. Put the tray under the grill, but at a distance from the heat; if the fish are too close, they will cook too quickly and may burn. Cook the fish for 5–6 minutes on each side until golden brown and cooked through; the flesh should flake easily when tested with a fork.

Remove the lemon slices from the mackerel and discard them. Transfer the fish to four serving plates, garnish with the couscous, spinach and preserved lemon I suggested, then serve.

Ingredients

4 x 300g whole mackerel, scales removed, gutted
1 lemon, thinly sliced
5cm piece root ginger, finely chopped
2 garlic cloves, crushed
juice of 2 lemons
2 tbsp chopped coriander
1 tsp paprika
1 tsp ground cumin
¼ tsp turmeric
4 tbsp Maldon sea salt

Serves 4

Rob Kirby

Chef Director, Lexington

Maldon sea salt-cured salmon
with beetroot and dill

Ingredients

1 x 1kg fresh salmon side,
 skinned and pin-boned
250ml fresh beetroot juice
125g Maldon sea salt
125g caster sugar
1 tsp ground black pepper
1 x bunch dill, chopped
250g long-sliced smoked salmon
1½ leaves of gelatine soaked in cold
 water

Serves 6–8

You'll need a 900g loaf tin or terrine mould. Cut the salmon side into bars 2.5cm thick and the same length as your mould.

Place the salmon bars in half the beetroot juice to colour for around an hour. Mix the Maldon salt, caster sugar, ground black pepper and half the chopped dill together in a large bowl. Then drain the salmon bars; roll them in the salt and sugar mix to coat them with it. Put the bars of salmon into a deep baking tray, cover with cling film and leave them in the fridge to marinate for 8 hours or overnight.

The next day, line the terrine mould with cling film, and then line it with the smoked salmon, allowing the ends to fall over the sides of the mould. Very gently warm the remaining 125ml of beetroot juice and melt the leaves of gelatine into the juice. Drain the salmon bars from their marinade, wash off any excess mixture and pat them dry with kitchen roll.

Finish your terrine by pouring a little beetroot juice in the bottom of the terrine, on top of the smoked salmon. Then lie the salmon bars on top and sprinkle them with chopped dill. Spoon over a little of the beetroot juice and melted gelatine mix. Repeat this layering process as the terrine fills to the top, then fold the smoked salmon ends over the top to seal it. Compress it with a weighted board and leave it to press overnight.

Serve with fresh horseradish and watercress salad.

Luke Matthews

Executive Chef, Chewton Glen

Wasabi-marinated salmon,
with pickled mooli and wasabi dressing

First, marinate the salmon. Put it on a large tray, plate or dish of the appropriate size. Put the Maldon salt and sugar in a bowl, and grind the juniper berries, peppercorns and coriander seeds in a food processor. Thoroughly mix them with the salt and sugar, then spread this mixture all over the salmon, turning it so that some is underneath. Marinate it for 36 hours, covered, in a cool place.

Prepare the pickled mooli. Bring the rice wine, sugar and chilli to the boil. Set this liquid to one side to cool; leave it to infuse for a while. Peel the mooli, cut it in half lengthways and slice it thinly, also lengthways. Toss the mooli in the pickling liquid at the last moment.

Blend all the ingredients for the wasabi dressing together. It should have a painting consistency; if it's too thick, let it down with a little warm water.

Wash the marinade off the salmon, and slice it finely. Arrange the sliced salmon on the plates then brush with the wasabi dressing. Scatter with some pickled mooli; I add a little white crabmeat and some diced mango, and finish it with micro coriander and black sesame seeds.

Ingredients

For the salmon and marinade:
1 x 1kg side of salmon
250g Maldon sea salt
200g sugar
20g juniper berries
20g white peppercorns
20g black peppercorns
20g coriander seeds

For the pickled mooli:
900ml rice wine vinegar
180g sugar
1 chilli, sliced
1 small stick of mooli

For the wasabi dressing:
1 tube of wasabi paste
juice and zest of 1 lime
25ml rice wine vinegar
25g honey
200ml peanut (groundnut) oil
75ml olive oil
a pinch of salt

To serve:
White crabmeat
Diced mango
Micro coriander leaves
Black sesame seeds

Serves 8–10, starter size

David Pitchford

Head Chef, Reads Restaurant with Rooms

Simple chilled gazpacho

Although this dish would be most appropriate for a summer lunchtime, I am told that it is an excellent remedy for a hangover at Christmas and New Year but, never having had a need for such a remedy, I have no way of knowing if this is true or not…

Ingredients

1kg ripe tomatoes
1 cucumber
2 large red peppers
100g onion, finely sliced
100g stale white bread,
  crusts removed
125ml extra virgin olive oil
75ml white wine vinegar
2 large cloves garlic, peeled
850ml iced water
Maldon sea salt
white pepper

Serves 10–12

Quarter the tomatoes, peel the cucumber and cut it into slices, quarter and de-seed the peppers and remove their stalks. Place the prepared vegetables and the sliced onion in a bowl with the bread, olive oil, vinegar, garlic and iced water. Season with Maldon salt and finely milled white pepper. Cover the bowl and put it in the fridge for 2 hours to marinate.

Then take the bowl out of the fridge and transfer everything to a blender (rather than a food processor, and you will need to do this in batches). Blend, and then pass through a medium strainer – not too fine – into a clean bowl. Push the liquid through the strainer with a ladle, and mix everything together well. Put the gazpacho in the fridge to chill once more, and serve it ice cold on a hot summer's day.

If you have time, serve the gazpacho with small bowls of garlic croutons, finely chopped onion, small cucumber dice, diced tomatoes (skinned and deseeded) and diced red, yellow and green peppers. These items should be served separately so that guests can help themselves to whatever they like.

Allan Picket

Head Chef, Plateau Restaurant

Twice cooked Harlequin squash soup
with Fourme D'Ambert croutons

At the Plateau Restaurant we use Secrett's Direct in Surrey for a lot of our winter vegetables. In early autumn their dinky squashes start coming through, and by mid season they will have up to fifteen different squashes of all shapes and sizes. One of my favourites is the Harlequin squash; it's versatile and the shell can be used as a serving bowl for soups and risottos if scooped out carefully. The acidity of the Fourme d'Ambert cheese works well with the sweetness of the squash, but other cheeses can also be used if you don't like a blue cheese. This recipe takes a little time to do, but the end result will amaze your guests.

Preheat the oven to 130°C/250°F/gas ½. Carefully cut the tops off the squashes, but don't throw them away. Take the bases and scoop the seeds out with a spoon. Sprinkle a little Maldon salt into each one and add a twist of the pepper mill, then place all four on an ovenproof tray, with the tops, and bake for 10–12 minutes (the tops may need a little less time, so check them earlier). Remove from the oven and leave to cool – this process will enable you to scoop the flesh out of the squashes a little more easily than when they are raw. Scoop out the flesh and set the shells to one side. Keep them warm.

Put the butter in a large pan over a medium heat, then add the onions and garlic and sweat them together for 3–4 minutes – do not allow them to colour. Add the scooped-out squash flesh, put a lid on the pan and cook it until it is soft, which should take about 5 minutes. Then add the milk and bring the soup to the boil, reduce the heat and then simmer for a further 5 minutes. I like my soups chunky, so just lightly blend with a hand blender until you have the desired consistency, and adjust the seasoning. Strain the soup if you prefer.

Increase the oven temperature to 160°C/320°F/gas 2–3 and prepare the cheese croutons while the soup is cooking. Slice the baguette, place the pieces on a tray and sprinkle them with a little olive oil. Bake them in the oven for 7–8 minutes until crisp and golden brown. Leave them to cool and then crumble the Fourme D'Ambert cheese over them.

When you are ready to serve, put the warm scooped-out squashes on serving dishes. Pour the hot soup into them, put the tops back on, place the croutons on the side – and serve immediately.

Ingredients

4 Harlequin squash
Maldon sea salt
black pepper
25g butter
1 onion, peeled and chopped
2 cloves of garlic, peeled
  and chopped
400ml semi-skimmed milk
1 small baguette (one day old)
100g Fourme d'Ambert

Serves 4

Dereck Quelch

Executive Chef, The Goring

Venison tartare

Ingredients

250g trimmed venison fillet
2 medium-sized beetroots, raw
about 150ml Cabernet Sauvignon
    vinegar
150ml olive oil
Maldon sea salt, to taste
Freshly ground black pepper, to taste
2 tsp chopped capers
2 tsp chopped gherkins
20g finely chopped shallots
zest of 1 medium orange
2 tsp chopped parsley
50g pasteurised egg yolk or
    3 egg yolks
4–6 tsp brandy
a splash of Tabasco, to taste
a splash of Worcestershire Sauce,
    to taste
50ml thick soured cream
2 tsp crushed black pepper

Serves 4

Peel the beetroot and cut it into fine slices approximately 1mm thick. Put these into a container and add Cabernet Sauvignon vinegar to cover. Set them aside for approximately 2 hours or until the beetroot softens.

Finely chop the venison. Remove the beetroot from the vinegar, draining it but retaining the vinegar, and arrange it in a neat circle on the serving plates. You want the venison to sit on top of this, with some of the beetroot visible, so judge it with a pastry ring and then use the same ring to form the venison.

Take 50ml of the retained vinegar liquor and mix it with the olive oil, Maldon salt and pepper, and set it aside. Now mix the venison meat with the capers, gherkins, chopped shallots, orange zest, chopped parsley and pasteurised egg yolk and brandy; add a splash of the Tabasco and Worcestershire Sauce to satisfy your own taste. Add Maldon salt and pepper to taste, as well.

Divide the tartare into 4 equal helpings and, using the ring, position the first portion so that it rests on top of the beetroot with some of the beetroot showing. Remove the ring and repeat this with the other portions.

Whisk the soured cream until it is thick, if necessary, and mix in the crushed black pepper. Place a spoonful of the cream on top of the venison. Make a dressing by shaking up the reserved oil and vinegar mixture, and drizzle a little around the plate, then serve immediately.

Richard Shepherd

Chef Patron, Coq d'Or Restaurant Company Ltd

Brommers' prawn salad

This is dedicated to my dear friend, journalist and ex-head of ITV Sport, John Bromley OBE, who wished life and food to be enjoyed without fuss… it's essentially a prawn cocktail on a plate. Eat it with chilled wine and warm company.

Make the Marie Rose sauce first. Deseed the tomato and chop it into small, pea-sized pieces. Put two teaspoons of these in a bowl and add the rest of the sauce ingredients. Mix well.

Rinse the prawns and squeeze them dry. Then chop the celery sticks to the same size as the tomatoes, and put the prawns and celery in a second bowl. Add the Little Gem lettuce and the mixed herbs. Then pour in the Marie Rose sauce and gently stir the salad to bind everything together.

Prepare the serving ingredients. Cut the tomatoes into wedges and season them with Maldon salt; cut the lemon into four wedges lengthways. Shake the olive oil and lemon juice together to make a dressing, and use it to dress the iceberg lettuce. Divide the iceberg between the serving plates and set the prawns on top. Then garnish with the ripe tomato pieces, the lemon wedges and a few fresh herbs. Serve immediately.

Ingredients

For the salad:
400g best-quality peeled
    and cooked prawns
2 sticks celery, peeled
1 Little Gem lettuce, shredded
a handful of mixed herbs,
    chopped: chives, parsley, chervil

For the Marie Rose sauce:
1 small tomato
100ml good-quality or home-made
    mayonnaise
25g tomato ketchup
2 tsp brandy
½ tsp Tabasco
1 tsp Worcestershire Sauce

To serve:
4 ripe tomatoes
1 tsp Maldon sea salt
1 lemon
3 tbsp olive oil
juice of half a lemon
a quarter of a large iceberg lettuce,
    roughly chopped
a few whole chives
a little parsley and chervil

Serves 4

Terry Tinton

Programme Manager, Senior Lecturer in Culinary Arts, Westminster Kingsway College

Roasted scallops
with Maldon sea salted cauliflower purée, pickle, bacon powder and rock chives

Ingredients

4 hand-dived scallops,
  sliced across twice (12 slices)
500g cauliflower, trimmed
  – 700g untrimmed weight
100ml white wine vinegar
50g granulated sugar
half a red chilli
200g unsalted butter
1 tsp Maldon sea salt
150ml single cream
3 thin slices pancetta
smoked Maldon sea salt, to taste
black pepper, to taste
butter for sautéing the scallops
a handful of rock chives, chopped
  (or ordinary chives if unavailable)

Serves 4

Cut a quarter of the cauliflower into tiny florets. Bring the vinegar to the boil, then add the sugar and chilli; decant into a bowl. Add the florets to this solution and steep them for an hour, allowing the liquid to cool naturally.

Cut the remaining cauliflower up roughly. Sauté it in a pan with half the butter and the teaspoon of Maldon salt. Once a little colour has been achieved, add the remaining butter and the cream, and cook gently for 10 minutes. Then blend the mixture into a purée and season to taste.

Dry fry the pancetta until it is really crispy, then blot off any oil or fat with a dry cloth or sheet of kitchen paper. Chop the slices and crush them to a powder in a mortar.

Season the scallops with a little smoked Maldon salt and pepper, and sauté them quickly in butter. To serve, arrange some cauliflower purée on the plate with the scallops. Garnish with the pickled cauliflower, powdered pancetta and rock chives.

Flavoured Maldon sea salts, page 70

Clockwise from top left: Lemon pesto salt,
Cumin seed salt, Ginger salt,
Olive salt and Five-spice salt.

Flavours and seasoning

Paul Gayler

Executive Chef, The Lanesborough

Flavoured Maldon sea salts

By using a great quality sea salt like Maldon as a base, you can create some wonderfully diverse flavours to enhance any foods – simply grind together flaked sea salt with interesting flavours. They make a great complement to meat, fish and vegetable dishes. Once made, keep the salts in airtight containers, ready for use.

Here are some of my personal favourites…

Cumin seed salt

This is wonderful for seasoning roast lamb, or vegetables such as roasted carrots or squash.

4 tbsp Maldon salt
4 tbsp cumin seeds

Heat the cumin seeds in a dry frying pan to lightly toast them for 30 seconds, keeping them moving to prevent burning. Transfer to a mortar or small coffee grinder, and add the salt. Blitz them to a fine grain. Use as required.

Lemon pesto salt

Great for roast fish or chicken.

2 tbsp prepared good-quality pesto sauce
4 tbsp Maldon salt
zest of one lemon

Preheat the oven to 50°C/120°F/the lowest possible gas. Mix the pesto in a bowl with the salt and lemon zest and stir them together well. Put the mixture in a small roasting tin in a flat layer and dry it in the oven for 1 hour. Allow it to cool, then store it ready for use.

Paul Gayler

Executive Chef, The Lanesborough

Ginger salt

Lovely for marinating fish, shellfish, etc.

4 tbps Maldon salt
4cm peeled root ginger, grated

Mix the Maldon salt and grated ginger together in a bowl and stir them well. Place the mix in a grinder and blitz it to a fine grain. Then transfer it to a roasting tin and proceed as for the lemon pesto salt.

Five-spice salt

Great for seasoning deep-fried fish or shellfish.

4 tbsp Maldon salt
1 tbsp Chinese five-spice mixture

Mix the Maldon salt and spice together in a bowl and store it ready for use.

Olive salt

Delicious for roast lamb or chicken, or to season roasted Provençal vegetables.

4 tbsp Maldon salt
2 tbsp stoned and chopped mild black olives

Place the Maldon salt and olives in a grinder, blitz them until fine and then store the mixture until you are ready to use it.

Other flavours could include chilli salt, smoked paprika salt, caraway salt, orange salt – the list goes on, so be creative!

Frances Bissell

Consultant Chef and Food Writer

Lavender salt

Ingredients

English lavender flowers
Maldon sea salt

Lavender salt is an unusual and subtle flavour enhancer for freshly cooked vegetables, served warm rather than hot. Green or white asparagus, new potatoes tossed in butter and a soft-boiled egg, all dusted with a little lavender salt – a gustatory delight. Sprinkle lavender salt on cod fillets cooked in olive oil with garlic. Season duck breasts with it after grilling them.

Because salt is a mineral, it has no volatile oils and flavour compounds to combine with other ingredients. You cannot, therefore, make a truly flavoured salt by 'infusing' it with another ingredient; lavender salt cannot be made by burying a few lavender sprigs in a jar of salt. Celery salt, for example, is made by grinding dried celery seeds with salt, and this is the method to use if you want lavender salt.

Use one part English lavender flowers to about ten parts Maldon salt. The flowers need to be absolutely dry otherwise they will cake with the salt. Grind them together in a mortar, or use a clean coffee grinder.

Paul Gayler

Executive Chef, The Lanesborough

Salt-preserved chilli peppers

Traditionally served as part of a mezze selection, these salt-cured chillies are wonderful served with dishes for the added kick!

Using a small knife, prick the chilli peppers all over so they will absorb the liquid marinade. Place the chillies in a 1 litre preserving jar, packing them down tightly.

Mix the remaining ingredients in a jug, then pour the liquid over the chillies. Seal the jar and store it in a dark place for up to one month, by which time the chillies will have softened and become pickled in flavour.

Ingredients

400g mild long chilli peppers
I dried small chilli
1½ tbsp Maldon sea salt
350ml water
120ml white wine vinegar

Paul Gayler

Executive Chef, The Lanesborough

Home-made preserved lemons

Preserved lemons are a staple in Middle Eastern cuisine, and they are often served with meat and poultry dishes. Usually they are prepared as whole lemons and preserved for months, rather than days. I also find them sometimes too aggressive, and so here is my slightly milder version.

Ingredients

10 lemons, thinly sliced,
   seeds removed
200g Maldon sea salt
2 tbsp sugar
5 garlic cloves, thinly sliced
3 bay leaves
1 tsp coriander seeds
½ tsp allspice berries
a little olive oil

Blanch the lemon slices in boiling water for 30 seconds, then drain them into a colander. Rinse them under cold water, then empty them onto a cloth and dry them well. Mix the Maldon salt and sugar together in a bowl, along with the garlic, bay leaves and spices. Stir everything well.

Layer the lemons in a 1 litre preserving jar alternately with the salt mix, pushing down the layers as you go. Seal the jar, then leave them to preserve for 3–4 days. Remove and store in a sealed container ready for use – serve them chopped in sauces, dressings, etc. They are used in the serving of my salt-grilled chermoula mackerel, for example (see page 53).

Frances Bissell

Consultant Chef and Food Writer

Toasted nut and lavender crunch (dhukka)

Toast the hazelnuts in a dry frying pan over a medium to high heat, stirring them so they don't catch. Once they begin to smell nice and toasted, put them into a bowl. Then repeat with the sesame seeds, putting them into another bowl, and again with the cumin and coriander.

Put the hazelnuts in a clean grinder and grind them briefly (on 'pulse'), until the nuts are broken up. Then add the rest of the ingredients and pulse again until the mixture is of roughly even size. It should be granular, not a powder or a paste.

Store it in an airtight jar in a cupboard. You can also make a larger quantity and store it in the freezer in airtight bags.

Ingredients

200g hazelnuts
100g sesame seeds
2 tsp Maldon sea salt
2 tsp lavender flowers
1 tbsp cumin seeds
1 tbsp coriander seeds
pinch of freshly ground black pepper

Billy Campbell

Executive Chef, Thistle Glasgow

Apple chutney

Ingredients

2kg apples
675g sultanas
1kg Demerara sugar
40g mustard seeds
675g shallots
175g Maldon sea salt
a large pinch of cayenne pepper
1.25 litres vinegar

Makes 10–12 jars

Peel and core the apples. Chop them up, and peel and chop the shallots too. Put them into a preserving pan or large casserole and add all the other ingredients. Bring to the boil – which will take time – and stir occasionally. Then reduce the heat a little so that the mixture simmers steadily, and cook it until thick: about 2 hours. Stir it regularly so that it doesn't catch during this time. It is ready when you can draw a wooden spoon through it and reveal the base of the pan for a few seconds, and should be well reduced in volume.

Ladle the hot chutney into warm sterilised jars (either heated in a low oven or put through the dishwasher) and fix the tops down at once. Don't forget to label and date your jars!

Hot-cured beef, page 96

To follow...

Salt baking is one of cookery's smartest, most beguiling parlour tricks. Every cook book tells you to be careful with the white stuff. To use a pinch. To season to taste. To know that you can only put in, not take out. And that's true. But then along comes the method for salt baking, like the great Albert Roux's stuffed sea bass in a Maldon sea salt crust which calls for nearly half a kilo of the stuff, or Jim Cowie's recipe for salt baked megrim sole, which demands double that. Yup. Well over two pounds of salt. Intuition, and a bit of culinary nous, tells you this will produce something close to a salt lick for cattle and certainly inedible to humans. Instead, the salt forms a hardened crust, with an internal seal, which keeps all the flavour in and all the saltiness out. It's also a lovely bit of theatre when you bring to the table something that looks like a lunar landscape and then crack it open to release the delicious smell of what's been hiding away cooking inside there.

Elsewhere in this section, these recipes prove the international language of Maldon sea salt. It may start life in the briny waters of England's Essex coast but here Maldon gets to travel. It plays a big part in Tony Cameron's venerable mutton curry (made to an Indian recipe dating back to 1861) or Billy Campbell's Mexican-influenced chilli beef. There's Kevin Cape's fiery-sounding larb gai from Thailand, and Alan Coxon's Mumbai-inspired tamarind and coconut fish curry. But not everything is exotica. Paul Heathcote gives us roast beef and Yorkshire pudding and Brian Turner offers up his killer recipe for roast chicken. However, if that all sounds a bit mundane there's always the novel-length pork belly recipe from the marvellous Jason Atherton of London's Pollen Street Social. Clear a weekend. Turn off the phones, roll up your sleeves and get cooking. It will be worth it.

Jay Rayner

Neil Thrift

Head Chef, Waldorf Astoria

Tian of lamb
with red wine butter sauce

Ingredients

4 x 180g canons of lamb

For the marinade:
50ml olive oil
15g crushed garlic
a small sprig of rosemary
a sprig of thyme
½ tsp black pepper

For the Anna potatoes:
4 Maris Piper potatoes
30g melted clarified butter
Maldon sea salt and freshly ground
    pepper
60g butter

For the ratatouille:
50ml olive oil
1 medium onion, finely chopped
10g crushed garlic
1 medium courgette,
    sliced and chopped
1 small red pepper, chopped
1 small green pepper, chopped
1 small aubergine,
    sliced and chopped
a small handful of basil,
    roughly shredded
3 tomatoes, peeled and deseeded
    (Ideally, you want roughly the
    same weights of onion, courgette,
    red and green peppers, aubergine
    and tomato – aim for about 90g of
    each)

Continued on next page...

Ask your butcher for larder-trimmed canons of lamb at around 180g each with all the fat and silver sinew removed. Mix all the marinade ingredients and marinate the meat, covered, in the fridge overnight.

To prepare the potatoes, peel and wash them quickly under the tap – don't soak them in water – then take a 3.5cm cutter and cut them lengthwise into four cylinders, or trim them to size. Slice the cylinders into discs around 2.5mm thick, and place the discs in a bowl with the clarified butter. Mix well, and add Maldon salt and black pepper. Set out a flat ovenproof pan and put four 7–8cm rings on it. Place the potato discs in a circular pattern inside the rings, each disc overlapping its neighbour. Divide the butter into four and place a piece in the centre of each ring. Drizzle olive oil around the outside of the rings and place the pan over a moderate heat. Keep the heat sufficient to give movement in the pan, but not so high that it burns the potatoes; don't rush it. When the outside turns golden brown, very carefully turn the rings over. Once the potatoes are browned on both sides, put the pan in the oven at 170°C/325°F/gas 3 until the potatoes are thoroughly cooked – around 30 minutes or so. Then leave them to cool under a light weight. When cooled, remove the potato discs from the pan, setting them out on a tray and covering until needed.

For the ratatouille, heat half the olive oil in a flat-bottomed pan. When the oil is hot, cook the onions and garlic until soft, then remove them from the pan and set aside to cool. In a little more of the oil fry off the courgette, cooking until al dente, then remove it from the pan. Repeat with the peppers, aubergine and tomato, cooking the latter until they start to break down. When all the ingredients are cooled, mix them together with the basil and cover.

To make the sauce, melt the butter in a pan. Add the shallots and the herbs, and cook them over a medium heat until they are soft but have not coloured. Add the alcohol, increase the heat and reduce the liquid by nine-tenths. Then add the gravy and bring the liquid back to the boil, reducing it by a further two-thirds. Check the seasoning and add Maldon salt to taste. Whisk in the butter a little at a time immediately prior to serving.

Continued on page 86...

Neil Thrift

Head Chef, Waldorf Astoria

For the sauce:
15g butter
60g chopped shallots
1 tsp thyme leaves
1 tsp finely chopped rosemary
500ml red wine
250ml port
100ml veal gravy, or chicken
    as an alternative
375g butter, cold in small cubes

For the garnish:
12 cloves of garlic, skin on
20ml olive oil
12 cherry tomatoes
240g cooked spinach leaves

Serves 4

Tian of lamb *Continued*

Prepare the garnish by frying the cloves of garlic for 1 or 2 minutes in the oil in an ovenproof pan, then roasting them in the oven at 180°C/350°F/gas 4 for about 10 minutes until the insides are soft. Add the cherry tomatoes to roast for 5 minutes and then remove both from the pan and leave to cool.

Remove the lamb from the fridge an hour before cooking and preheat the oven to 180°C/350°F/gas 4. Heat up a frying pan and, when smoking, add a little of the oil from the marinade. Season the meat, put it in the pan and seal until the canons are golden brown on both sides. Transfer them to the oven, roasting for 8–10 minutes depending on the degree of cooking preferred. Start reheating all the other elements of the dish, either in the oven or on the hob. Remove the lamb from the oven when it is cooked to your taste and keep it warm.

Using the rings from the Anna potatoes, form a layer of spinach leaves. Top them with the potatoes, then top the potatoes with the ratatouille. Garnish each plate with three cherry tomatoes and garlic cloves. When the lamb has rested, carve it into slices and arrange these on top of the ratatouille. Pour the sauce around the dish, and serve.

Jason Atherton

Chef Patron, Pollen Street Social

Twenty-four hour pork belly
*with fermented apple, seeds and nuts and
a beer sauce*

Remove the skin from the pork belly and set it to one side. Mix the sel rose, Maldon salt, star anise, cinnamon, peppercorns and cloves together well and rub them all over the belly, then put the belly in a dish, cover and put it in the fridge overnight, along with the skin. Preheat the oven to 85°C/185°F. Put 3 litres of the duck fat in a large casserole, add the belly and confit it for 18 hours. Then remove it from the confit, press it gently and chill it for a further 8 hours.

Prepare the pork floss. At the same time as you are confiting the belly, confit the skin separately in a litre of the duck fat infused with the thyme, garlic and some more Maldon salt until it is well over-cooked. Remove the skin from the confit and allow it to cool down on a rack so excess fat drains away. Once the skin is cool, put it onto a baking tray and dehydrate it in the oven at a low temperature until it is very dry; this will take several hours. Dry the skin further on paper, and keep changing it; this will help the process and dry the skin as much as possible. Once it is dry, increase the oven temperature to the maximum possible, season the skin well and put it into the oven on a tray until very well puffed up. Then dry it out again, once more as much as possible, and blend it in a Thermomix (or pulse it, in stages, in a heavy-duty spice grinder) until you have a fine powder.

Make the sauce. Using a very large pan over a medium heat, colour the pork trimmings and chopped shallots in the olive oil. Then deglaze the pan with the sherry vinegar. Add the white wine, thyme, peppercorns and bay leaf, and reduce the liquid to a syrupy consistency. Add the beer and reduce it down again – skim the surface well. Then add the malt barley syrup and reduce again. Finally, add the stock and bring to the boil. Then reduce the heat to a simmer, skimming as before, and cook the sauce out for 30 minutes. Pass it through a fine sieve and chill.

Continued on page 88…

Ingredients

For the pork belly:
500g pork belly
4 litres duck fat
20g miso paste

For the salt cure and pork floss:
30g sel rose
70g Maldon sea salt,
    plus a little for the pork floss
5 star anise, crushed
3 cinnamon sticks, crushed
1 tsp peppercorns
15 cloves, crushed
a handful of thyme
2 cloves of garlic,
    peeled and crushed

For the pork beer sauce:
500g pork trimmings
4 banana shallots, chopped
2 tbsp olive oil
half a head of garlic
a handful of thyme
a small bay leaf
10 white peppercorns
25ml sherry vinegar
half a bottle of white wine
1 x 330ml can English ale
50ml malt barley syrup
1 litre brown chicken stock

To serve:
extra virgin olive oil

Contined on next page…

Jason Atherton

Chef Patron, Pollen Street Social

For the fermented apple purée:
500g Granny Smith apples
10g fresh yeast
1 tbsp lemon juice
2 tsp sugar
250g butter

For the seed and nut mix:
100g Puy lentils
100g pearled spelt grains
1 small carrot, chopped
1 stick of celery, chopped
1 small white onion, chopped
50g pumpkin seeds
30g sesame seeds
30g hazelnuts
30g sunflower seeds
1 tsp coriander seeds,
   toasted and ground
a splash of soy sauce
Maldon sea salt to taste
1 tsp sugar
a little extra virgin olive oil

To serve:
buttered spring cabbage

Serves 4

Twenty-four hour pork belly *Continued*

Peel the apples and slice them thinly; put them in a large sealable bag. Blitz the yeast, lemon juice and sugar and add them to the apple. Then seal the bag and leave it in a warm place for 30 minutes. Remove the apple mixture and sweat it rapidly in the butter until tender, then blend the mixture until smooth – a hand blender is ideal. Pass it through a sieve into a bowl, check the seasoning and keep it warm. Discard the apple which remains in the sieve.

A short while before you are ready to serve, prepare the seed and nut mix. Rinse the Puy lentils and check them over for small stones. Put three times their volume of water in a pan. Then add the lentils, spelt grains, carrot, celery and onion and bring to the boil; reduce the heat and cook until tender. Toast the pumpkin and sesame seeds, hazelnuts and sunflower seeds in a dry pan, then add the ground coriander seeds and a splash of soy sauce, and stir well. Season with the Maldon salt and sugar. Drain the lentils and spelt, and mix in the seed and nut mixture. Check the seasoning, and serve immediately, adding a little olive oil just beforehand.

Cut the pork belly into four portions. Just before serving, glaze the pork bellies with a mixture of 100ml of the sauce and 20g miso, mixed well together, and reheat them in a warm oven. Reheat the sauce and split it with some extra virgin olive oil. Divide the apple purée between the serving plates, and place the pork belly to one side. Add some of the lentil and seed mixture, then pour some sauce around the dish. Scatter some pork floss over it and serve, accompanied with buttered spring cabbage.

Tony Cameron

Chef de Cuisine, The Oriental Club

Mutton curry

This recipe is based on a recipe from **Indian Cookery** *by Richard Terry, chef de cuisine at the Oriental Club in 1861…*

Remove any excess fat from the mutton and cut up any large pieces. Set it aside.

Using a large pan over a medium heat, dry roast the cumin seeds until the scent rises, then add the onions and ghee. Sweat the onions to soften them, stirring from time to time. Make a paste with the turmeric, paprika, garam masala, chilli powder and a little water. Add this to the onions and allow it to cook out for a few minutes. Add the mutton, grated garlic and ginger, and the piece of cinnamon stick and mix everything together.

Chop the pineapple and the chilli very finely together until they are almost puréed and add them to the pan. Then add the chopped tomatoes, tomato purée, Maldon salt and pepper and stir them in. Mix together the vinegar and jaggery or Demerara sugar and add those to the pan too. Stir everything thoroughly, and add the water.

Bring to the boil, remove any scum and reduce the heat. Allow the curry to simmer gently until the mutton is tender – how long this takes will depend on the size of the pieces, but allow at least 90 minutes to 2 hours. During cooking, check the curry every so often and add a little more water if necessary. Check the seasoning.

Serve with steamed Basmati rice, perhaps a vegetable curry, naan bread, sambals, chutneys and raita…

Ingredients

1kg diced mutton
1½ tsp cumin seeds
2 large onions, sliced
30g ghee
1 tsp turmeric
1½ tsp paprika
1 tsp garam masala
½ tsp chilli powder
1 clove garlic, grated
1 cube of fresh ginger, about 1.5cm, grated
half a cinnamon stick
1 slice of fresh pineapple
1 red chilli
150g chopped tomatoes (skinned, if using fresh)
1½ tsp tomato purée
1 tbsp Maldon sea salt
1 tsp cracked black pepper
2 tbsp red wine vinegar
2 tsp jaggery or Demerara sugar
600ml water

Serves 4

Billy Campbell

Executive Chef, Thistle Glasgow

Rossdhu chilli beef

This is delicious served with guacamole, sour cream and tacos, or in griddled tortilla wraps…

Ingredients

500g rump of beef,
  chopped into small dice
5 tsp oil
2 medium onions, diced
2 large chillies, diced with
  the seeds in (or more, to taste)
4 large garlic cloves, chopped
225g tinned chopped plum tomatoes
5 tsp tomato purée
Maldon sea salt
1½ tsp ground cumin
chopped fresh coriander, to garnish

Serves 4

Put the oil in a large saucepan over a medium to high heat. Add the beef, diced onions, chillies and garlic and sweat them together. Drain off any excess fat if a lot comes off the beef. Drain the chopped tomatoes, but reserve the juice. Then add the chopped tomatoes and tomato purée to the pan, and a pinch of Maldon salt. Continue cooking for 10 minutes; if there's any sign of it catching, add a little of the juice from the tomatoes. Add the cumin and cook for a further 10–20 minutes, or until the beef is tender. Put it in a serving bowl, check the seasoning and top with some coriander.

Kevin Cape
Executive Chef, Shook Restaurant

Spicy minced chicken salad
(Larb Gai)

First make some roasted rice. Soak the basmati rice, then drain it well and roast it in a dry frying pan until it begins to colour. Grind it in a mortar and set to one side.

Mince the chicken with Maldon salt and garlic. Heat the stock in a medium pan, and season with salt (check the taste first as some stocks are quite salty) and sugar. Add the chicken mince and cook gently, stirring frequently until just cooked, about 3–4 minutes. Be careful not to overcook it or the meat will toughen. Season with lime juice, chilli powder and fish sauce. Mix in the shallots and herbs, then stir in the spring onion and the finely chopped chilli; keep a little aside for a garnish if you wish.

Check the seasoning – the salad should taste hot, sour and salty – and adjust accordingly. Sprinkle with the roasted rice and pine nuts. Serve with raw vegetables such as cabbage, snake beans and cucumber.

Ingredients

300g skinless chicken breast
  or thigh fillets
1 tbsp basmati rice
a pinch of Maldon sea salt
1 small garlic clove, finely chopped
  (optional)
3 tbsp fresh chicken stock
an extra pinch of Maldon sea salt
a pinch of white sugar
3 tbsp lime juice
½ tbsp roasted chilli powder
1 tbsp fish sauce
3 red shallots, sliced
a handful of mint and coriander
  leaves, chopped
2 tbsp shredded pak chii farang
  (long-leaf coriander)
4 tbsp spring onion, sliced
1 tbsp finely chopped chilli padi
  (bird's eye chilli, or to taste)
Pine nuts, to garnish

Serves 4

Professor Peter A. Jones MBE

Director of Wentworth Jones, tourism and hospitality specialists

Hot-cured beef

There are a number of different methods for salt baking meat. Part cooking, part curing, this recipe results in remarkably tender, delicious meat. This recipe comes from Farzan Contractor, Executive Chef of the Meat and Wine Company, and originally appeared in **The Salt Book** *(Arbon Publishing, 2010). I'm grateful to the publisher and chef for allowing me to use it.*

How many it serves depends on how you use it!

Ingredients

250g juniper berries
1kg Maldon sea salt
150g of sugar
olive oil
1 beef tenderloin, about 2kg in weight

In a dry frying pan, lightly toast the juniper berries, then crush them in a mortar. Put them in a large bowl and mix them together with the Maldon salt and sugar, then sprinkle a little olive oil over the mix to moisten it. Preheat the oven to 180°C/350°F/gas 4.

Trim the tenderloin of any fat, then pat it with a kitchen towel until it is completely dry. Take a baking tray and spread some of the salt mixture on it – enough to allow the tenderloin to sit entirely upon it. Put the tenderloin on the mix and use the rest of the salt to completely cover the meat, ensuring that no part is visible.

Bake for 20 minutes, and then turn the oven down to 40°C/100°F (or an equivalent very low temperature) and let the meat cook for a further 30 minutes. Remove it from the oven and immediately break off all the salt so that the meat is clearly visible. Wrap the tenderloin tightly in muslin and let it sit overnight in a cool dark place.

Once the beef has been cured it can be served either hot or cold. As with cured Wagyu beef, it may be sliced thinly and served with a simple dressing and herbs, accompanied by crusty bread. Alternatively you can cut it into thick slices, grill the slices and bring them up to temperature, and serve with mashed potatoes, green beans and a favourite sauce.

Philip Corrick

Executive Chef of Clubhouses, Royal Automobile Club

Canape di polenta con funghi trifolati

(Polenta with forest mushrooms trifolati)

Make the polenta first. Bring the water and Maldon salt to the boil in a heavy-bottomed pan. Pour in the maize flour in a steady stream, and stir it with a wooden spoon until it thickens. Let it cook slowly for at least 30 minutes, and keep stirring so that it doesn't catch; it should be thick and fully cooked. Pour it into a terrine mould or other suitable lined container, and set it aside to cool completely before you start cooking the mushrooms.

Put the butter and oil in a sauté pan over a medium heat; add the shallots and cook them gently until they are opaque. Then add the mushrooms and cook for a couple of minutes until soft. Add the garlic and white wine and increase the heat to reduce the liquid by three-quarters. Lower the heat and add the cream; cook the mixture and reduce the liquid once more, until it has the consistency of a sauce. Season with milled pepper and Maldon salt and finish with the chopped parsley.

Remove the cold polenta from its tin, cut it into squares and sauté it in a little oil. Place a slice of polenta in the centre of a serving plate and spoon on the mushrooms. Decorate the dish with sprigs of parsley, lightly sprinkle with Maldon salt flakes, and serve.

Tip: All the preparation for this dish can be done in advance. The mushroom mix can be reheated, but you must take care to cool it after making – and do not put the parsley in if you make it in advance. Leave that until you reheat it.

Ingredients

For the polenta:
750ml water
a pinch of Maldon sea salt
120g yellow maize flour
  (or polenta, but not 'easy cook')
cooking oil

For the creamed wild mushrooms:
25g butter
2 tbsp olive oil
80g shallots, chopped
500g mixed wild mushrooms,
  cleaned and sliced
1 clove garlic, crushed
150ml dry white wine
250ml double cream
black pepper
Maldon sea salt
1 tbsp chopped parsley

Serves 4

Jim Cowie

Chef Patron, Captain's Galley Seafood Restaurant

Maldon sea salt-baked megrim sole

Ingredients

1.5kg whole megrim sole,
  cleaned and washed
1kg Maldon sea salt
2 egg whites
1 lemon
extra virgin olive oil for drizzling
garlic, basil, bay leaf, or whatever
  fresh herbs you have handy

Serves 4

Preheat the oven to 220°C/425°F/gas 7. In a bowl, stir together the Maldon salt and egg whites until they are well combined and have the consistency of wet sand. Take a large baking sheet and spread half of the salt mixture into a rectangle just larger than the megrim sole. Put the fish on top. Halve the lemon crosswise and cut three slices from one half, reserving the remaining half. Insert the slices of lemon and herbs into the cavity of the fish. Pat the remaining salt mixture over the fish to cover it completely (you can leave part of the head clear of salt if you want to use a temperature probe to check when it is ready) and bake it in the middle of the hot oven for 20–25 minutes.

Take it out of the oven and rap all around the edge of the salt crust with the back of a large spoon to loosen it. Then lift the top off. Debone the fish: lift the meat from the fish and put it onto a serving platter. Squeeze the juice from the reserved lemon half over the fish and drizzle with a little oil. Scatter a few herbs over the dish and serve immediately.

Tip: If you wish to trim off the salt skin before serving that's fine, but if you want the wow factor, serve the fish with the salt intact, crack it and do the work at the table. It's simple.

Paul Gayler

Executive Chef, The Lanesborough

Maldon smoked sea salt roasted potatoes
with rosemary butter

I love the delicacy of flavour in Maldon smoked sea salt. Here I use it to roast some baby new potatoes – a real treat – to serve with any roast or grilled meat.

Preheat the oven to 200°C/400°F/gas 6. Place half the smoked Maldon salt in a dish large enough to take the potatoes lying flat on the base. Cover the salt with the potatoes, and then cover the potatoes with the remaining salt, packing it down around them. Drizzle the water liberally over the salt, then place in the preheated oven and cook for 40–50 minutes. After this time, remove the dish and leave it to sit for 10 minutes.

Meanwhile, mix the butter in a bowl with the remaining ingredients. Remove the potatoes and rub off the salt crust thoroughly using a cloth. Cut them in half, place in a serving dish, top with the butter mixture and serve immediately.

Ingredients

450g new salad potatoes,
Juliette for example
750g–1kg smoked Maldon sea salt
   (depending on the size of the dish)
600ml water
100g unsalted butter
2 tbsp freshly chopped rosemary
1 tsp grated lemon zest
1 shallot, finely chopped

Serves 4

Alan Coxon
Managing Director, Coxon's Kitchen

Fish in a tamarind and coconut curry

Ingredients

300g white, meaty fish such as monkfish, with all skin and bone removed, cut into equal-sized chunky pieces
groundnut or other neutral oil for frying

For the batter:
100g besan (chick pea) flour
1 tsp cardamom seeds, lightly crushed
¼ tsp Maldon sea salt
1 tsp freshly ground black pepper
200–250ml cold water
3 tbsp fresh coriander, chopped

For the sauce:
4 tbsp rapeseed oil
1 onion, finely chopped
2 tomatoes, chopped
250ml coconut milk
½ tsp Maldon sea salt
¼ tsp freshly ground black pepper

For the spice seasoning:
75g grated coconut
4 dry chillies
1 tsp cumin seeds
½ tsp turmeric
2 tbsp tamarind pulp extract
1 x 2cm piece of fresh ginger, peeled and finely grated
3 cloves garlic, crushed
¼ tsp Maldon sea salt

To serve:
fresh lemon wedges
a sprinkling of Maldon sea salt
a handful of freshly torn coriander

Serves 2 as a main course, or 4 as a starter

Make the batter by sifting the flour into a bowl with the cardamom, Maldon salt and freshly ground black pepper. Add the water a little at a time, whisking as you go, to form a smooth, lump-free batter. Then add the chopped coriander, stir and set aside to rest for a few minutes.

Mix together all the spice seasoning ingredients using either a blender or a pestle and mortar. Rub the seasoning into the fish until it is well coated, then leave it aside for a few minutes for the seasoning marinade to flavour the fish.

Meanwhile, make the sauce. Put the rapeseed oil in a heavy-based pan over a medium heat. Once it is hot, add the onion and cook it gently until it becomes translucent, but not brown. Add the chopped tomatoes, followed by the coconut milk and seasoning, then bring to a gentle simmer.

While the sauce is cooking, heat some neutral-tasting oil ready for frying in a large pan or deep-fat fryer. Then place the fish into the batter, turning it to ensure all its surfaces are well coated. Gently shake off any excess batter before lowering the fish into the hot oil and frying it. Cook the fish through; the batter will be crisp and golden. When the fish is ready, remove it from the oil and drain any excess oil off on kitchen paper.

Serve the fish with the sauce (this may be served as it is, with a slightly chunky texture, or sieved for a smoother sauce consistency), some lemon and a scatter of Maldon salt and fresh torn coriander leaves. Basmati rice makes a good accompaniment.

Mark Dodson

Chef Proprietor, The Mason's Arms

Cod with Maldon sea salt
with a tomato and thyme vinaigrette

Skin and pin bone the cod fillets, and put them in a dish where they can be laid out flat. Cover them with Maldon salt and put the dish aside for 45 minutes. Take the fillets out, shake off as much salt as possible, then rinse the fish under running water.

Put the milk, thyme and bayleaf in a large pan over a medium heat and poach the cod; how long this takes will depend on the thickness of the fillets, but it shouldn't be longer than 6 minutes. Remove the cod from the poaching liquor and drain off any excess.

Make the tomato vinaigrette when you are ready to serve. Combine the tomatoes, thyme sprigs, tomato juice and sherry vinegar in a liquidiser (or use a hand blender). Then gradually add the oil. Pass the liquid through a fine sieve and use immediately, pouring a little around the pieces of fish.

Tip: At the Mason's Arms, we serve this dish with crushed new potatoes and chorizo julienne. Just before serving we add the julienne of chorizo to the potato and put the potato in the middle of the plate, then place the cod on top of the potato, with the tomato vinaigrette around it. A little Maldon salt is sprinkled over everything, and it is garnished with a few rocket leaves.

Ingredients

4 x 150g cod fillets
250g Maldon sea salt
500ml milk
1 large sprig of thyme
1 bay leaf

For the tomato vinaigrette:
150g tomatoes, skinned
  and deseeded
5 small sprigs of thyme
100ml tomato juice
10ml sherry vinegar
75ml olive oil

Serves 4

Peter Fiori

Executive Chef, Coutts Bank

Saddle of Iberian Pork
with trompette mushrooms and pea purée

Ask your butcher to French trim the rack of pork and score the fat.

Ingredients

For the pork:
1 x 2.5–3kg part saddle or rack of
  Iberico pork on the bone, to serve
  8; if Iberico unavailable, choose
  rare breed or organic pork
10g dried trompette mushrooms
  (dried ceps if unavailable)
10g Maldon sea salt
1 tsp Dijon mustard

For the pea purée:
300g peas
50g butter
1 shallot, diced
1 tbsp double cream
10 mint leaves
Maldon sea salt and black pepper,
  to season

For the rosti:
85g butter
500g waxy potatoes
a little additional butter, for cooking

To garnish:
100g fresh trompette mushrooms
  (oyster mushrooms, sliced, if
  trompettes unavailable)
a little butter
pork jus

Serves 8

Preheat the oven to 180°C/350°F/gas 4. Grind the dried mushrooms and Maldon salt together in a spice mill or coffee grinder, then season the meat and brush the Dijon mustard all over the skin. Rub the mushroom and salt mix all over the mustard until you have achieved a dark coating. Roast the meat for approximately 2½–3 hours, until it has reached an internal temperature of 54°C, or to taste.

While the pork is cooking, prepare the pea purée. Bring a pan of water to the boil, add the peas and blanch them briefly, then set them aside. Melt the butter in a heavy-based pan over a medium heat and sauté the diced shallot until it is soft and transparent, but not coloured. Add two-thirds of the blanched peas, cook them together and then purée them using a liquidiser or hand blender. Add the cream and mix that in, then add the mint leaves and the rest of the peas. Check the seasoning, set it aside and keep it warm.

When the meat is done to your taste, take it out of the oven and put it to one side to rest for 10 minutes.

Just before the meat is ready, start preparing the rosti. Melt the butter. Peel and grate the potatoes, then dry them by putting them in a clean cloth and squeezing out the water. Transfer to a bowl, season with Maldon salt and pepper and mix in the melted butter. Heat a heavy-based frying pan, then stand four plain metal rings in it (cook the rosti in two batches and keep them warm). Press some of the potato mixture inside each ring to make a neat shape and press it down; slide a little knob of butter down the side as the rosti cooks. When the underside is golden – after about 2 minutes – remove the ring and flip each rosti over carefully. Cook the other side for a further 2–3 minutes until crisp. At the same time, lightly sauté the fresh trompettes in a little butter.

To serve, spoon the pea purée on each plate and top with a slice of pork through the bone. Place a rosti on top of the pork at an angle, garnish with the sautéed mushrooms and a little pork jus.

Paul Gayler

Executive Chef, The Lanesborough

Herb-baked chicken in a Maldon sea salt crust

Cooking food under a salt crust really captures the natural flavours, and doesn't make it as salty as you might imagine (you don't eat the crust). Crack the crust open at the table to release the wonderful aromas in front of your guests…

Make the crust first. Mix the flour, Maldon salt and mixed herbs in a bowl. Make a well in the centre of the mix; add the egg and water. Using your hands, bring it together to form a dough. Cover the bowl with cling film and leave it in the fridge to rest the dough for 30 minutes.

Preheat the oven to 200°C/400°F/gas 6. Season the chicken breasts with Maldon salt and pepper, then roll them in the chopped garlic and herbs.

Take the salt-crust dough out of the fridge and roll it out to about 5mm thick. Cut it into quarters. Wrap a chicken breast in each piece, enclosing everything except the wing bone. Brush the egg glaze liberally over the surface of the dough and place the wrapped breasts on a large baking sheet. Bake them in the oven for 18–20 minutes, and leave them to stand for 2 minutes before serving.

Ingredients

4 x 180g free-range chicken breasts, on the bone
Maldon sea salt and black pepper
2 garlic cloves, crushed
2 tbsp chopped mixed herbs – thyme, rosemary, etc

For the crust:
450g plain flour
100g Maldon sea salt
1 tbsp mixed chopped herbs, as above
1 large egg
175ml water
a little beaten egg, to glaze

Serves 4

Paul Heathcote

Proprietor, PH Restaurants Ltd

Roast beef and Yorkshire pudding

Ingredients

For the beef:
1.5kg sirloin of beef, off the bone
Maldon sea salt and freshly milled
    pepper
½ tsp curry powder
2 carrots, peeled but whole
2 onions, peeled, cut in half
4 cloves of garlic, lightly crushed
a small bunch of thyme, in sprigs
a little olive oil
about 250ml water
125ml glass of red wine
2 tsp cornflour, dissolved in a little
    cold water

For the Yorkshire pudding:
375ml semi-skimmed milk
3 eggs
150g plain flour
a pinch of Maldon sea salt
2 tbsp oil, dripping or fat from
    the joint

Serves 6

Preheat the oven to 220°C/475°F/gas 7. Season the beef well with Maldon salt and freshly milled pepper, and sprinkle the curry powder over it. Put it to one side. Place the carrots and onions in a roasting tray along with the beef, and scatter the garlic and thyme over it. Drizzle some olive oil over, and add a little water to the roasting tray.

Place in the oven and cook for 55 minutes–1 hour 10 minutes, or depending on how pink you want your beef. Keep topping up the tray with a little water just to prevent the contents from burning.

While the meat is cooking, prepare the Yorkshire pudding. Put the milk into a liquidiser and break in the eggs. Add the flour and Maldon salt on top and gradually liquidise everything well. Select a Yorkshire pudding tray, or separate tins, add some of the dripping from the roasting tin and heat the tray or tins in the oven. Turn the oven up to its highest point. Pour in the batter to come about two-thirds of the way up the tins and cook for approximately 10 minutes until well risen. When you take the beef out, turn the oven down to 160°C/315°F/gas 2–3 and cook for a further 5 minutes until golden and well cooked.

Remove the beef to a tray or plate and cover loosely with a little foil. Sieve the juices from the roasting tin into a saucepan and put it over a medium to high heat. Add the red wine, bring to the boil and thicken with a little dissolved cornflour. Skim off any fat and serve the gravy with the beef and the Yorkshire puddings.

Herbert Berger

Sea bass baked in a Maldon sea salt crust

with Asian spices and a ginger, lime and wasabi beurre blanc

Mix all the salt crust ingredients, except the optional egg white, together well. It's best to prepare this dry mix two to three days in advance so it can infuse; just store it in an airtight container. It will keep for the next time, too.

Dry the sea bass well and stuff it with all the ingredients for the filling, making sure they are evenly spread out inside it.

Preheat the oven to 200°C/400°F/gas 6. You will need a sheet of silicone or parchment paper 70cm x 50cm in size; fold it so that you have a sheet of about 35cm x 50cm. Fold or crimp up the edges so they form a little lip and place the sheet on a flat baking tray.

Mix the egg white into the salt mix (it will help to hold the crust together, giving you a harder crust and enabling you to mould it to shape, but alternatively you could simply spray the fish with water once you have finished covering it with the mix). Put a layer of the salt mix in the middle of the paper the size and shape of the bass. Very carefully place the fish on top. Cover it completely with plenty of the salt. Bake it in the oven for about 35–45 minutes. Test it with a probe to make sure the inside is hot.

Make the beurre blanc while the fish is cooking. Place the shallots, wine and vinegar in a stainless steel pan over a high heat and reduce until only a few tablespoons of liquid are left. Lower the heat slightly and whisk in the cold butter piece by piece, whisking constantly until you have a velvety beurre blanc – remove the pan from the heat just before adding the last piece of butter. Add all the other ingredients except the lime juice and wasabi and let them infuse while the bass is baking. Keep the sauce warm, preferably by putting the pan in a bain-marie, a container of warm water – but not too warm, or the sauce may split. Adjust the seasoning just before serving and add the lime juice and wasabi. Strain the sauce through a fine sieve just before serving.

To serve the bass, crack open the crust and divide the fish between the plates; serve with the perfumed beurre blanc.

Ingredients

1 x 1–1.5kg sea bass, gutted and scaled

For the salt crust mix:
1.5kg Maldon sea salt
1 heaped tbsp coriander seeds
1 level tbsp black peppercorns
½ tbsp Szechuan peppercorns, slightly crushed
½ tbsp fennel seeds
12 cardamom seeds, slightly crushed
10 star anise
1 egg white, beaten (optional)

For the filling:
1 stick lemongrass
3 sprigs fresh coriander
2 lime leaves, cut in half
5 thin slices fresh ginger
1 mild red or green chilli, split in two and deseeded

For the beurre blanc:
50g Thai shallots, finely chopped
1 glass of Sancerre
½ glass white wine vinegar
250g unsalted butter, cut into small cubes and refrigerated
2 sprigs coriander
1 tsp chopped lemongrass
half a lime leaf
1 heaped tsp chopped sushi ginger
juice of 1 lime
½ tsp wasabi paste

Serves 4

Martyn Nail

Executive Chef, Claridges

Lemon, ricotta and basil gnocchi *with Maldon sea salt-baked baby beetroot and goat's curd*

Cooking beetroot like this, baking them with Maldon salt, locks in their natural moisture so they cook from within. They stay beautifully moist and retain all their natural flavour, which is enhanced by the seasoning of the salt. I like to cook this dish for my friends in the spring and summer months, reminding me of my travels in Italy.

Ingredients

For the gnocchi:
350g floury (baking) potatoes
1 large egg, beaten
a pinch of nutmeg
350g ricotta
zest of 1 lemon
a few basil leaves
200g flour
Maldon sea salt, to season
black pepper, to season
30g butter

For the beetroot:
8 baby beetroots (or 2 regular size, if you can't find smaller ones)
150g Maldon sea salt
1 tsp black peppercorns
several sprigs of thyme
2–3 cloves of garlic, unpeeled and crushed

To serve:
a splash of balsamic vinegar
a splash of olive oil
a squeeze of lemon juice
30g ricotta
60g goat's curd
200g peas, cooked lightly
200g broad beans, shelled and cooked lightly

Serves 4

Begin by baking the potatoes for the gnocchi. Preheat the oven to 180°C/350°F/gas 4. Scrub the potatoes and bake them in the oven until cooked through, which will probably take about an hour. You can test them by sticking a knife in; if it comes out easily, with no resistance, they are ready.

Lower the oven to 150°C/300°F/gas 2 for the salt-baked beetroot. Wash the beetroot and trim off the leaves if still attached, but do not peel. Take two large sheets of foil and lay them out like a cross. Put the Maldon salt in the middle, and add the peppercorns, thyme and garlic. Place the beetroot on the salt. Lift the foil up a little, add one tablespoon of water and pull the foil together, closing it around the beetroot but not too tightly – they need room to steam. Put them on a baking tray and then cook them in the oven for about 30–40 minutes, or until soft (if you're using two larger beetroots instead of the baby ones this will take longer – allow twice the time). Unwrap the beetroots as soon as they are cool enough to handle and gently rub off the skins; when they are cooked and still warm the skins should rub off easily. Discard the skins and the salt mixture, then set the beets aside.

This part is key. While the potatoes are still warm, just cool enough to handle without actually burning yourself, peel off the skins or use a spoon to scoop out the cooked flesh. While it is still warm it needs to be mashed in a ricer, with a potato masher or even passed through a coarse sieve into a large bowl – it should look like grated potato. After this it will have cooled down more, but it shouldn't be completely cold. Fold the beaten egg into the potato, then add the nutmeg, ricotta, lemon zest, a couple of torn basil leaves, and enough flour to bind the mixture. Season with Maldon salt and

Martyn Nail

Executive Chef, Claridges

pepper and knead the dough a little, adding more flour if the mixture is too loose. Lightly flour a work surface and tip the dough out onto it. Finish kneading the dough by hand – it should be light and dry to the touch. Then divide it into long sausage shapes. Cut them into pieces the size of large walnuts. For an authentic finish, roll these down the back of a floured fork.

Put a large pan of salted water on to boil, and then reduce the heat to a steady rolling simmer. Blanch the gnocchi in the water in batches (don't overfill the pan as they need room to float up) for 3–4 minutes until firm; they will rise to the surface when ready. Lift them out with a slotted spoon, drain them briefly on kitchen paper and then set them to one side to cool and dry.

When you are ready to serve, halve the beetroots and warm them up in a pan with a little balsamic vinegar. Put the butter in a large non-stick pan and fry the gnocchi briefly, browning them quickly on all sides. Put a dash of olive oil and a squeeze of lemon in another pan and toss together the warm peas, broad beans, a little of the ricotta and goat's curd, and season with Maldon salt and pepper. Place half of this in the bottom of each serving bowl and build up with the pieces of baby beetroot, then a few small spoons of the goat's curd, the pan-fried gnocchi, a little more pea mixture and a few torn basil leaves. Serve immediately.

Tip. The best potatoes to use are those that are low in moisture and high in starch, so choose potatoes which are advertised as 'bakers' or 'good for baking' in your local shop. If you have some older potatoes, they are actually ideal – they will have lost some of their moisture. And note that the potato needs to remain warm while you're working so it doesn't become gluey from all the starch.

Allan Picket

Head Chef, Plateau Restaurant

Braised venison
with pomegranate

Ingredients

1.2kg piece venison haunch
(boned)
1 bottle full-bodied red wine
2 cloves garlic, peeled
1 large carrot, roughly chopped
1 stick celery, roughly chopped
half a medium onion, roughly
chopped
2 juniper berries, crushed
3 litres good quality brown veal stock
a pinch smoked Maldon sea salt
seeds from 1 pomegranate, to serve

Serves 4

Cut the venison into 5cm dice. Put the red wine in a large bowl with the garlic and the chopped vegetables, then add the venison. Cover and leave overnight in a cool place to marinate.

The following day, drain off the wine and transfer it to a pan. Bring it to the boil and reduce the quantity by two-thirds. Pass this through a sieve lined with a cloth so there is no sediment in your sauce once it is made, and set it to one side.

Preheat the oven to 150°C/300°F/gas 2. Separate the cubes of venison from the vegetables, and pull out the cloves of garlic as well. Heat a large casserole dish and roast the venison until golden brown. Then add the vegetables and colour them until they are golden brown too. Finally add the garlic, juniper berries, the strained and reduced wine marinade, and the veal stock. Bring to a simmer and cover the casserole with a cartouche of greaseproof paper and a tightly fitting lid. Transfer it to the oven and cook for around 3 hours, until the meat is tender to the touch.

Pour off most of the stock into a pan, then bring it to the boil and reduce it for a sauce. Keep the remaining braise hot, and once you have the required consistency pour the liquid back over the meat and vegetables. Season the venison with a pinch of smoked Maldon salt.

Serve, garnished with pomegranate seeds.

Tip: Depending on the time of year we have this dish on the menu, we change the garnish from pomegranate to poached quince…

Ben Purton

Executive Head Chef, The Royal Horseguards Hotel and One Whitehall Place

Rump of Casterbridge lamb
with Maldon sea salt-baked shallot tarte Tatin, and a thyme and rosemary jus

Preheat the oven to 180°C/350°F/gas 4. Start by preparing the tartes Tatin; you will need 4 x 10cm Tatin moulds. Mix together the Maldon salt, thyme and rosemary, and sprinkle onto a baking tray big enough to hold all the shallots in one layer. Place the shallots on the salt and bake for approximately 20 minutes until slightly softened. Remove from the oven and allow to cool until you are able to handle them. Carefully peel off the skins.

Brush the Tatin moulds with the softened butter and season them well with salt and pepper. Arrange 6 shallots in each mould, and press down slightly so that they are at an even depth. Then top with the puff pastry circles, tucking the pastry in at the sides so the shallots are completely covered. Brush the pastry with the olive oil, prick it over with a fork and bake in the oven for about 20–25 minutes, until golden and slightly risen. Remove them from the oven and rest for 2–3 minutes before carefully turning them out. Keep them warm until you are ready to serve.

Heat the olive oil in an ovenproof sauté pan. Season the lamb well with Maldon salt and freshly milled black pepper. Put the rumps into the pan and colour them well on all sides. Then place the pan in the oven for 2–3 minutes. Remove the pan, turn the meat over and add the garlic, thyme and rosemary. Return the pan to the oven for another 6–8 minutes. Remove from the oven, lift the lamb out of the pan and leave it to rest in a warm place for 3–4 minutes. Pour off any excess oil or fat from the pan, and return it to the hob over a high heat. Add the stock and reduce it by half until the juice has the consistency of a sauce. Take the pan off the heat, whisk in the butter and pass the sauce through a fine strainer into a jug.

To serve, place a Tatin on each serving plate, slice each rump of lamb into five even pieces and lie them on the plate next to the Tatin. Spoon the pan juices over, and serve with some steamed broccoli or green beans.

Tip: Cooking the shallots over salt intensifies the flavours, making the shallots even sweeter, and adding the herbs also infuses some extra flavour into the shallots. Seasoning the Tatin moulds cuts into the sweetness ever so slightly. And lamb can take a fair bit of seasoning, especially when using Maldon rather than table salt.

Ingredients

For the lamb:
4 x 200g rumps of lamb
1 tbsp good olive oil
1 clove of garlic, unpeeled but
    lightly crushed
2 sprigs of thyme
2 sprigs of rosemary
200ml good quality stock
    (brown, lamb or chicken)
15g unsalted butter

For the Tatin:
24 medium shallots, unpeeled
200g Maldon sea salt, with a little
    reserved for seasoning
2 sprigs of thyme
2 sprigs of rosemary
1 tbsp salted butter, softened
Freshly milled black pepper
4 x 10cm rounds of rolled-out puff
    pastry, approximately 2.5mm thick
1 tbsp good olive oil

To serve:
Steamed broccoli or green beans

Serves 4

Gary Rhodes

Restaurant Associates UK, 4th Floor

Ingredients

For the duck seasoning:
2 star anise
2 tsp paprika
2 tsp coriander seeds
2 tsp ground ginger
1 tsp Chinese five spice powder

For the pasties:
500g duck breast meat, trimmed
   and diced
100g shredded beef or vegetable
   suet, chilled until very cold
50g cold foie gras, diced (optional)
50ml goose/duck fat
   (plus an extra 50ml, if needed)
2½ tsp duck seasoning
3 tsp Maldon sea salt
good twist of milled pepper
85g dried cranberries, chopped
2 sheets of puff pastry
1 egg
1 egg yolk

Makes 12–15 pasties

Duck and cranberry pasties

Place all the duck seasoning ingredients in a spice mill or coffee grinder and blitz them to a fine powder. Then pass it through a fine sieve for a smooth finish. Store it in an airtight container until you are ready to go.

Mince together the duck breast meat, suet and foie gras (if using), putting them through the medium dye of a mincing machine. Chop them very finely indeed if you don't possess a mincer, or pulse them briefly in a food processor. Put the mixture in a bowl.

Over a medium heat, melt the goose or duck fat gently; don't let it get too hot. Add the melted fat, all the seasonings and dried cranberries to the duck mixture, and work them in well until they are completely mixed together. Pass through the fine dye of a mincing machine twice.

Lightly flour the worktop and roll out the pastry, dividing it into approximately 15cm squares before brushing lightly with egg wash (made from the egg plus the extra yolk; whisk until loose and set aside any that is left over), covering the pastry. Place a tablespoon-sized ball of duck mixture towards the centre of each square, folding the pastry over and creating a triangular shape. Carefully press around the edges to seal the pasty completely. A cutter, using the 'rolled' edge, can be lightly pressed around the ball, leaving a neat finish. Put the pasties on a non-stick baking sheet and refrigerate to set. Then cut around the ball, leaving a small border.

Preheat the oven to 190°C/375°F/gas 5. Egg wash the pasties again before baking them for 26–28 minutes until they are a deep golden brown. Halfway through cooking rebrush with egg wash and sprinkle them with a touch of Maldon salt.

Rick Stein

Chef Proprietor, The Seafood Restaurant

Fried fish in Panko breadcrumbs

Dredge a fish fillet through the flour and knock off the excess, then dip it in the beaten egg. Hold it up to drain off any excess egg, and place it in the breadcrumbs. Turn the fish over until the fillet is evenly coated with a good layer of crumbs and set it to one side. Repeat with the other fillets. You can put the breaded fillets into the fridge to firm up the breadcrumbs if you wish.

You will need to preheat the oil in a large pan to 180ºC to fry the fish. If you do not have a frying thermometer, take a large breadcrumb and drop it in the fat; when it sizzles, starts to colour and rises to the surface the oil is ready. Fry the fish in the oil for 3 minutes or until light and golden, depending on the thickness of the fillets. Drain them on pieces of kitchen paper to remove any excess fat.

Sprinkle the fish with Maldon salt, and serve immediately with lemon wedges and tartare sauce.

Ingredients

4 white fish fillets, such as lemon
    sole, plaice, haddock or cod
100g plain flour
2 eggs, beaten and seasoned
    with salt
250g Panko breadcrumbs
Maldon sea salt
oil for frying

Serves 4

Albert Roux

Maître Cuisinier de France, Consultant Chef and Food Writer

Stuffed sea bass with fennel
cooked in a Maldon sea salt crust

Ingredients

1 x 1kg filleted sea bass

For the Maldon sea salt crust:
2 tbsp fresh thyme leaves
1 tbsp fresh rosemary leaves.
   finely chopped
450g Maldon sea salt
2 large egg whites
150ml cold water
300g plain flour

For the stuffing:
1 large fennel bulb
half an onion, finely chopped
2 tbsp olive oil
180ml double cream
1 tbsp pastis (e.g. Ricard)
1 tsp cornflour

For the side vegetables:
6 baby new season onions
   (grelot onions)
3 tsp olive oil
2 sprigs of thyme
1 bay leaf
salt and pepper
150ml dry white wine
100ml water
100g cep mushrooms,
   cleaned and sliced
6 dried tomatoes, chopped

Serves 6

Make the crust first. In a bowl, mix the herbs and Maldon salt together. Add the egg white and cold water, then add the flour and knead to form a firm dough that is not too moist or sticky. Cover with cling film and leave to rest for 3–4 hours at room temperature.

Scale the fish and remove the eyes and gills. Snip off the fins with a pair of heavy-duty scissors. Remove the pin bones with a pair of tweezers, then rinse the fish in cold water and dry it off.

Prepare the stuffing. Finely chop half the fennel. Sweat the onion with the olive oil for 5 minutes. Add the fennel and cook for a further 3–4 minutes, stirring occasionally, until nearly tender. Pour in the cream, turn up the heat and reduce until it starts to thicken. Mix the pastis with the cornflour until smooth; pour into the boiling fennel mixture and whisk well for 15 seconds, then remove from the heat. Season well – it doesn't need much salt as the salt from the crust flavours everything – and set aside.

Heat the oven to 200°C/400°F/gas 6 and put a baking sheet in the oven to heat up. Place the fish on a large sheet of lightly oiled greaseproof paper or cling film and fill it with the creamed fennel stuffing. Roll the dough out until it is large enough to encase the fish. When you are ready to bake, pick the stuffed fish up using the paper or film, and roll it onto the dough. Slide off the paper or film and wrap the fish in the dough, ensuring all seams are well sealed. Brush with egg wash and bake for 18–20 minutes; the crust should be a light golden brown. Allow the fish to rest for 15 minutes before serving.

While the fish is resting slice the remaining fennel lengthways into 5mm slices. Peel the baby onions and, if they are bigger than a marble, cut into halves or quarters. Put the onions and fennel with a teaspoon of the olive oil in a smoking hot, wide, thick-based pan. Cook until well browned, turning occasionally. Add the thyme and bay leaf; season well. Add the wine and bring to the boil, then add the water and turn the heat down. Cover with greaseproof paper and simmer gently for about 12 minutes, until the vegetables are tender but still a little crunchy. Meanwhile, sauté the mushrooms in the remaining olive oil and add to the fennel and onions. To finish the vegetable garnish, add the dried tomatoes and a swirl of extra virgin olive oil.

Bring to the table in the pan. Serve the fish in the salt-crust parcel, and open it at the table to release the aromas.

Brian Turner, CBE

President of the Academy of Culinary Arts

Roast chicken
with spring onion and tomato

This is a simple and tasty dish, but buy the best chickens you can – free range, organic...

Get your butcher to create the crowns of chicken for you, or do it yourself. Remove the legs and put them aside for later use. Take out the wishbone from each crown.

Preheat the oven to 200°C/400°F/gas 6. Melt the butter in a pan over a medium heat, add the spring onions and chopped garlic and sweat them gently together; do not allow them to colour. Then add the tomatoes, season with black pepper and a little salt. Stir, then remove the pan from the heat and allow the mixture to cool.

Gently separate the skin from the flesh over the breasts of the chicken crowns from the wishbone end, using your fingers to make a pocket over each breast; try not to make a hole when you do this. Put the tomato mix into the pockets formed, and then pull back the skin to give the chicken its original shape.

Mix the Maldon salt with the cumin seeds. Put the chicken crowns into a roasting tin. Splash them with oil, sprinkle with the salt and cumin seed mixture, and roast them until they are cooked – between 40 and 60 minutes, depending on weight.

Take the crowns out of the oven and keep them warm, allowing them to rest for at least 10 minutes while you make the gravy. Pour the excess fat out of the roasting tin and put the tin on the heat. Add the white wine to the fat that remains in the tin and bring it to the boil. Reduce the liquid by two-thirds, then add the stock and continue boiling until the liquid has reduced by half. Check for seasoning, then add the cold butter and shake it in. Sieve the gravy into a clean pan and add the parsley; warm it gently when you are ready to serve.

Carve the chicken and serve it with the gravy.

Tip: To see if your chicken is cooked properly, pierce the thickest part with a skewer or the point of a sharp knife. The juices should run clear. However, you should try to catch the bird just before this happens. I always like to leave my chicken to rest for about 10-20 minutes before carving, when it will continue to cook slowly in its internal heat.

Ingredients

2 crowns of chicken, from birds
   about 1.3kg–1.5kg each
25g butter
2 spring onions, chopped
1 clove garlic, chopped
2 tomatoes, deseeded and chopped
black pepper and salt to season
1 tbsp Maldon sea salt
1 tsp cumin seeds
1 tbsp olive oil
1 glass dry white wine
300ml chicken stock
25g cold butter, finely chopped
1 tbsp parsley, chopped

Serves 4

David Sharland

Executive Chef, The Seafood Restaurant

Roast potatoes
with Maldon sea salt

Ingredients

1.5kg potatoes (such as Maris Piper)
1 tsp Maldon sea salt
250g goose fat
1 sprig each thyme and rosemary
Garlic cloves to taste – optional

Serves 4

Preheat the oven to 200°C/400°F/gas 6. Peel the potatoes and cut them into three or four pieces, then rinse them. Place the potatoes in a large pan, cover with water and add 1 teaspoon of Maldon salt. Bring to the boil and simmer for 10 minutes or until the potatoes are almost cooked.

Drain the potatoes in a colander, and leave them in it; give them a good shake. The potatoes need to be shaken up to give them a rough exterior without breaking them up, as this will give them a crispy outside when cooked.

Melt the goose fat in a pan. Place the potatoes in a heavy roasting pan and cover them with the fat. Add the sprigs of herbs and the optional garlic and roast for 40 minutes or until golden brown. Serve hot – with plenty of Maldon salt.

Nick Vadis

UK Executive Chef, Compass Group UK & Ireland

Baked sea bream
with salted macadamia crumb and a braised fennel, tomato and caper dressing

Preheat the oven to 180°C/350°F/gas 4. Cut the fennel lengthways through the root and trim out the tough core. Put the fennel halves in a small ovenproof dish. Add the capers, lemon juice, olive oil and white wine vinegar, then season with some Maldon salt and pepper. Cover the dish with foil and bake it in the oven until the fennel is soft and cooked – how long this takes will depend on the size of the bulb, but will probably be about 30–40 minutes; check after 20 to see if it is softening. Once it is cooked, set it aside and keep it warm.

Deseed the tomatoes and quarter them; chop the parsley and add half to the tomatoes. Set these aside and make the crumb mixture. Mix the chopped macadamia nuts with the breadcrumbs and the rest of the chopped parsley, then add some Maldon salt and pepper to taste. Lightly oil an ovenproof dish, place the fillets of sea bream in it, skin side down, and cover the fish with the crumb. Drizzle a little oil over, and bake in the oven for approximately 10 minutes, or until the fillets are cooked.

To serve, spoon some of the cooked fennel and capers onto each plate. Add the tomatoes, place the fish on top, and drizzle some of the cooking liquor from the fennel over and around the dish. Finally, add the whole roasted macadamia nuts to add flavour and another texture to the dish.

Tip: If you wish, a little coarse Maldon salt sprinkled over the crumb just before serving will add even more texture and seasoning...

Ingredients

4 fillets of sea bream
1 fennel bulb
20g capers
juice of 1 lemon
50ml olive oil
50ml white wine vinegar
6 cherry tomatoes
20g flat leaf parsley
80g macadamia nuts, chopped
60g breadcrumbs
40g macadamia nuts, whole,
  roasted in a dry frying pan
Maldon sea salt, to season

Serves 4

John Williams

Executive Chef, The Ritz London

Fillet of turbot
with baby leeks, broad beans and morels

Ingredients

For the fish:
4 x 150g thick fillets of turbot
Maldon sea salt
40ml olive oil
40g butter

For the sauce:
50g shallots
2 sticks of celery, trimmed
40g celeriac
1 medium leek
100g butter
half a bottle of Champagne
250ml excellent chicken stock
50ml excellent vegetable stock
200ml double cream
juice of half a lemon

For the cauliflower cream purée,
used in serving:
half a cauliflower
500ml milk
50g butter
100ml cream

To serve:
24 baby leeks
300ml chicken stock
50g butter
pepper and Maldon sea salt, to taste
16 large morels
60g broad beans, cooked and shelled
200g cauliflower cream purée

Serves 4

Begin with the sauce. Finely chop the shallots, celery, celeriac and leek. Melt the butter in a pan over a medium heat and sweat the vegetables for a few minutes until they are soft but have not coloured up. Add the Champagne, bring to the boil and reduce the liquid until almost syrup-like in consistency. Then add the stocks to the pan and reduce the liquid by half. Add the cream, bring the sauce to the boil, reduce the heat and simmer for 5–10 minutes. Pass the sauce through a fine sieve into a clean saucepan, season with pepper and Maldon salt and finish with the juice of half a lemon. Keep it warm.

For the cauliflower purée, cook the cauliflower in the milk and enough water to cover until it is tender. Drain it thoroughly, then put it in a liquidiser with the cream, butter and seasoning. Blend to a smooth purée, season to taste and keep warm.

Cut the fish fillets into squares and season them with Maldon salt. Sauté the fish in olive oil and butter until golden brown and just cooked. While the fish is cooking, cut the baby leeks down to 5cm long and cook them briefly in the chicken stock with butter, pepper and Maldon salt. Remove the stalks from the morels and sauté the tops in butter; add a little stock or consommé to braise them until tender.

To serve, spoon the cauliflower purée onto the centre of each plate. Dress the turbot on top, then place the leeks and shelled broad beans on top and the morels on top of them. Now add the sauce. Either drizzle it elegantly over the dish, or aerate it with a Bamix and spoon the resulting foam over the fish. Serve immediately.

John Williams
Executive Chef, The Ritz London

Butter-poached lobster
with ginger and cauliflower cream purée

Begin by preparing the sauce. Blanch the lobsters in boiling water for 20 seconds to release the flesh away from the carcass. Carry on cooking the claws for a full 2 minutes so the flesh may be released from the shell, then refresh in iced water. Break the head away from the body, then crack the tail to remove the shell from the tail meat. Repeat the process with the claws and knuckle (sturdy scissors are useful for opening up the lobster). Clean the head and any grey matter and reserve the coral to use in the sauce later. Chop the shell into small, equally sized, pieces.

Heat a heavy saucepan and sauté the shell in the butter until it roasts lightly and becomes red in colour. Add the onion, carrot and celeriac and sweat them for approximately 10 minutes, then add the fennel, ginger, cardamom, coriander seeds and leaves (retain a few) all together. Cook them slowly to allow the perfume to develop, and be careful that they don't catch. Then flambé with the brandy, allowing it to totally vaporise, and reduce to a fine glaze. Add the lobster and chicken stocks and slowly cook them down, reducing the liquid by three-quarters. Add the cream, bring to the boil slowly, then lower the heat and simmer gently for 10 minutes.

Season the sauce to taste and pass it through a fine sieve (or chinois) and finish by whisking in the coral, which has also been passed through a sieve. This must be done away from the heat or it will curdle the sauce. Keep the sauce warm.

For the cauliflower purée, cook the cauliflower in the milk and enough water to cover until tender. Drain it well, then place in a liquidiser with the cream, butter and seasoning. Blend to a fine smooth purée and season to taste.

To cook the lobster, bring the clarified butter up to a temperature of approximately 65°C. Put the lobster portions in the butter and poach them very slowly for 5 minutes. Then lift them out and drain onto kitchen paper.

To serve, place a spoonful of cauliflower purée in the centre of the plate and rest the lobster on top. If you can, foam the sauce with the aid of a Bamix mixer and pour it generously over the lobster; otherwise, drizzle the sauce elegantly around and over it. Finish with a few leaves of coriander.

Ingredients

4 x 500g British lobsters
100g butter
I small onion, finely chopped
1 carrot, finely chopped
quarter of a small celeriac,
   finely chopped (about 40g)
quarter to half a bulb of fennel,
   chopped (about 40g)
small piece of root ginger, chopped
6–8 cardamom pods
10 coriander seeds
 small bunch of fresh coriander
60ml brandy
250ml lobster or fish stock
125ml chicken stock
25ml double cream
pepper and Maldon sea salt, to taste
250g clarified butter

For the cauliflower cream purée:
half a cauliflower
500ml milk
50g butter
100ml cream

Serves 4

David Simms

UK Executive Chef, Restaurant Associates / Roux Fine Dining

Cured Cornish mackerel
with oyster cream, charred baby leeks,
pickled radish and sea vegetables

Ingredients

4 mackerel fillets, pin-boned
50g Maldon sea salt
3 tbsp caster sugar
zest and juice of 1 unwaxed lemon
1g fennel pollen
8 baby leeks
olive oil
200g mixed sea vegetables
  (such as sea aster, stonecrop,
  sea beet)
2 breakfast radishes
50ml pickling liquor
1 rock oyster
1 egg yolk
100ml grapeseed oil

For the pickling liquor:
100ml Chardonnay vinegar
75ml water
1 tbsp caster sugar
2 pink peppercorns
1 star anise
sprig of thyme
pinch of Maldon sea salt

Serves 4

Begin by preparing the pickling liquor. Mix all the ingredients together in a pan and bring to the boil. Simmer for 5 minutes then remove from the heat and allow to cool. Store the liquor in an airtight jar.

Trim the mackerel fillets. Mix the Maldon salt, sugar, lemon zest (set the juice aside) and fennel pollen together and spread the mix on a small tray or in a dish large enough for the fillets to lie flat and side-by-side. Then place the mackerel fillets on top, flesh side down. Cover the tray or dish with cling film and put it in the fridge for 8 hours.

Prepare the vegetables. Trim and clean the baby leeks, dress lightly with oil and seasoning and place in a very hot dry frying pan until heavily charred on one side. Remove them from the pan and allow them to cool at room temperature. Trim and wash all the sea vegetables, then blanch and refresh them individually in iced water. Slice the radishes thinly (on a mandolin if possible) and place them in 50ml of the cold pickling liquor for 15 minutes. Then drain them well.

Make the oyster cream just before you are ready to serve. Shuck the oyster and place it in a jug with all its juice. Add half the lemon juice – retain the rest – and the egg yolk, and blitz with a hand blender until smooth. Then very slowly add the grapeseed oil, still blending but gently, until thick and glossy. Check the seasoning and pass the cream through a fine sieve or chinois into a bowl, and refrigerate

To serve, remove the mackerel from the fridge and lift the fillets off the salt mix. Give them a light rinse in running water, then pat them dry. Cut each mackerel fillet in half lengthways. Dress all the vegetables (except the radish) with a little olive oil and a splash of lemon juice, then season with Maldon salt. Put a dessert spoon of the oyster cream just off the centre of the plate and swipe it with a pallet knife. Arrange the two pieces of mackerel on the plate, overlapping with the dressed vegetables. Finish with the pickled radish and a drizzle of olive oil.

Chefs' twists and tips

Here are some quick tips for instant culinary success from our top chefs.

"Use a mixture of sea salt, smoked sea salt and crushed black pepper for seasoning steaks for your barbecue." – Allan Pickett

"Maldon is versatile; if I'm using it for seasoning meats I prefer to use it as it is, but for pastry work I like to grind it down to a finer form." – Billy Campbell

"When serving cheese, accompany it with Maldon sea salt and caramel walnuts. To make these, coat walnuts lightly in a stock syrup; lightly salt them and bake for 6 minutes in the middle of an oven preheated to 200°C." – Daniel Richardson

"Add extra Maldon sea salt to your cooking water for bright green vegetables such as asparagus, broccoli, etc. Before use, refresh the cooked vegetables in icy cold water – this will ensure they stay bright, crisp and green." – James Chapman

"If you wish to firm up a piece of fish prior to cooking, sprinkle the surface with Maldon sea salt 30 minutes before cooking. When you're ready to cook, wipe off the salt and pat the fish dry. You won't need to season again." – Jim Cowie

"Chop garlic mixed with Maldon sea salt on a board to make a paste. Transfer to an airtight jar and cover with olive oil. This will keep for a couple weeks and can be used to season your cooking." – Lawrence Keogh

"Use Maldon sea salt to add texture to a dish. I love the crunch!" – Mark Dodson

"Adding salt to meat before pan frying or grilling is good; the salt helps caramelise the natural sugars in the meat, sealing in the flavour and moisture and forming a natural crust on the exterior of the meat." – Paul Gayler

"I sprinkle Maldon sea salt on chocolate tarts as the clean, pure flavour of Maldon sea salt helps emphasise the sweetness and richness of chocolate." – Regis Negrier

"Always sprinkle the salt on focaccia just before placing it in the oven. If sprinkled on before this the salt will melt and leave blotches on the focaccia when baked." – Stefano Borella

"When using Maldon sea salt remember it is not as dense as granulated salt so you may need to use more. Don't be afraid of natural salt in food. Yes, we need to monitor levels, but salt enhances flavour and can make food taste better." Steven Walpole

"Maldon sea salt tip – never run out of it." – David Pitchford

Pot de crème au chocolat, page 157

To finish...

There was a time when the use of salt in sweet things was restricted pretty much only to Brittany, which has a long tradition of selling salted butter caramels. But bit by bit it became hip: salty sweet things were picked up by the big name chefs in Paris, and made into macaroons by master pastry chef Pierre Hermé. Next it crossed the Channel. In the late 1990s Heston Blumenthal began serving a sublime block of soft salted caramel as part of a complex dessert at his restaurant The Fat Duck. Soon the new wave of chocolatiers was running with the idea, creating versions both hard, soft and liquid, so that if you weren't paying attention it dribbled down your chin. They began selling chocolate bars sprinkled with flakes of sea salt so that you got a distinct crunch with your chocolate rush. Finally the use of the white stuff with melted sugar went mainstream, turning up in mass-produced ice creams and chocolate bars. During the 2008 US presidential election, even Barack Obama admitted it was salted caramel chocolates that were getting him through the arduous campaign.

The curious thing is that, as anyone who has ever made an apple crumble knows, a pinch of salt has always been the killer ingredient for desserts. It's there in the best of those crumble toppings, not to mention in various cake and biscuit recipes. It gives a sublime lift to flavours. Often in this selection of recipes, however, the salt really does take centre stage, be it in William Curley's dark chocolate mousse with a Maldon sea salt caramel centre, Claire Clarke's chocolate tart with salted caramel and candied peanuts or Ben Purton's glorious-sounding Maldon salted dark chocolate fondant with Maldon salted caramel and macadamia ice cream. After all, why have salt only once in a dessert, when you can have it twice?

Jay Rayner

Benoit Blin

Head Pastry Chef, Le Manoir aux Quat'Saisons

Chocolate crumble
with lemon butterscotch sauce and hazelnut ice cream

This is a different way to make a yummy chocolate tart or crumble. In this recipe the addition of the salt to the crumble – and in particular the caramelised hazelnuts for the garnish and in the ice cream – will enhance the flavour and lower the overall sweetness of the dish. Bon appétit!

Ingredients

For the salted caramel hazelnuts and paste:
120g caster sugar
40ml water
400g hazelnuts, coarsely crushed
   and sieved to remove powder
2 pinches of Maldon sea salt
another 1–2 tsp water, optional

For the salted hazelnut ice cream:
6 egg yolks, from medium organic
   eggs (120g in weight)
80g caster sugar
350ml milk
150ml whipping cream
10–15ml Kirsch
a pinch of Maldon sea salt
hazelnut paste, as above

Continued on next page...

First, prepare the salted caramel hazelnuts and paste. In a large pan, bring the sugar and water to a thick boil, to around 115°C. Fold in the crushed hazelnuts and a pinch of Maldon salt. Mix until the hazelnuts are completely coated in the caramel. Pour onto a greased tray to cool. When cold, keep half for the garnish later on and turn the other half into a paste using the Thermomix on medium speed. If you do not have a Thermomix, you will need to do this in a blender or food processor; add a couple of teaspoons of water.

Now for the salted hazelnut ice cream. Pour all the ingredients into the Thermomix, on the top of the hazelnut paste already prepared, and cook it on medium speed to 82°C. Cool it down over an ice-water bain-marie to stop further cooking, then churn it in an ice-cream machine.

Alternatively, pour the milk into a heavy-based pan and heat slowly; do not boil. Leave the milk to cool a little. Whisk the egg yolks and sugar together until thick and creamy, then gradually whisk the milk into the eggs. Strain this mixture back into the pan and cook it over a low heat. Add the hazelnut paste along with the Kirsch and stir until they are fully integrated into the custard. Chill a large bowl in a container filled with ice cubes. When the custard is thick enough to coat the back of a spoon, strain it into the chilled bowl and push any remaining paste through the sieve. Allow to cool, then whisk in the cream until evenly blended. Pour the ice-cream mixture into a shallow container and place it in the freezer. Whisk it two or three times in the next hour or two to break down the ice crystals as they form.

Continued on page 144…

Benoit Blin

Head Pastry Chef, Le Manoir aux Quat'Saisons

Chocolate crumble *Continued*

For the crumble:
75g unsalted butter, cold
75g Demerara sugar
25g almond powder (optional)
a pinch of Maldon sea salt
55g flour
15g Valrhona cocoa powder

For the chocolate cream:
165ml whipping cream
70ml full-fat milk
1 medium organic egg, beaten
155g 70% Valrhona chocolate,
   roughly chopped into small pieces

For the lemon butterscotch sauce:
180g whipping cream
150g caster sugar
20ml water
75ml liquid glucose
75ml lemon juice, heated
1 tsp grated lemon zest

Serves 8

For the crumble, cut the butter into cubes and store in the fridge until very cold. In a food processor, mix all the other ingredients together until the crumble has the texture of breadcrumbs. Set it aside in the fridge or freezer for a minimum of 30 minutes before use. Preheat the oven to 170°C/325°F/gas 3. Sprinkle the mixture evenly into a 20cm tart ring on a baking sheet covered with greaseproof paper and bake for 8–9 minutes. Once out of the oven, carefully place an 18cm ring on top, press down slightly into the crumble without cutting through, and set it aside to cool.

Now make the chocolate cream. In a medium-sized saucepan, bring the cream and milk to the boil. Whisk gradually onto the beaten egg. Pour half over the chocolate and stir gently with a whisk until the chocolate is completely melted and the cream is smooth. Add the remaining milk and cream. Pour it into the 18cm ring on top of the crumble base and leave it to set in the fridge for at least 2–3 hours.

To make the lemon butterscotch sauce, bring the cream to the boil. Meanwhile, in a deep pan, heat the sugar, water and glucose until they become a blond caramel. Carefully pour the hot lemon juice and zest on top, followed by the hot cream – poured slowly. Stir well, and bring the mixture back to the boil for 1 minute, then cool it down quickly over an ice-water bain-marie; the sauce should be amber yellow in colour. Put it in the fridge.

When everything is set, remove both rings from around the crumble and the chocolate cream, heating the rings up with a small blowtorch for a professional finish. Cut the tart into portions, put onto the serving plates, and sprinkle the lemon sauce and the caramelised hazelnut over the top. Serve with a quenelle of salted hazelnut ice cream.

Albert Roux

Maître Cuisinier de France, Consultant Chef and Food Writer

Poached pear in caramel
with Maldon sea salt caramel ice cream

Begin by preparing the ice cream. Put the 250g sugar in a heavy pan over a moderate heat and stir until it begins to melt, then allow it to caramelise and reach a deep amber colour. Off the heat, add the cream and milk carefully; replace the pan on the heat and stir until the caramel has dissolved. Cream the egg yolks and the 55g of sugar together. Pour this over the milk mixture and cook at 90°C, stirring with a spatula. Pass the liquid through a fine sieve or chinois, add the Maldon salt and chill it in a bowl over ice. Turn the mixture into an ice-cream maker and churn, following the manufacturer's instructions.

Now make the caramel syrup in which to poach the pears. Cook half the sugar to the caramel stage, as above. Add the water and cook until dissolved, then add the remaining sugar and bring it to a simmer.

Peel the eight pears but leave the stems attached. Put the pears in a pan with the liquid caramel syrup and split vanilla pod. Cover with greaseproof paper and gently simmer until just tender, then allow to cool. When the pears are cold, slice the top half off, and core out the centres.

While the whole pears are cooling, make the pear coulis and the pistachio tuiles. For the coulis, make a syrup with the sugar, water and vanilla, then add the chopped pears. Simmer until they are soft and most of the liquid has evaporated. Mix and pass through a very fine sieve or a tamis. Set aside.

Continued on page 146…

Ingredients

For the poached pears:
8 pears
1 vanilla pod, split

For the Maldon sea salt caramel ice cream:
250g sugar
125g whipping cream
750ml milk
1½ tsp Maldon sea salt
10 egg yolks
55g sugar

For the caramel syrup:
500g sugar
1 litre water

For the pear coulis:
100ml water
100g sugar
zest of 1 lemon
2 vanilla pods
6 pears (Williams), peeled, cored and chopped

For the pistachio tuiles:
150g sugar
3 large egg whites
60g butter, melted
2 tbsp plain flour
75g shelled and unsalted pistachios, coarsely chopped

For the caramel sauce:
200g caster sugar
400ml double cream

Serves 8

Albert Roux

Maître Cuisinier de France, Consultant Chef and Food Writer

Poached pear in caramel *Continued*

For the pistachio tuiles, preheat the oven to 180°C/350°F/gas 4. Whisk the sugar and egg whites together until the sugar has dissolved. Add the butter and then the flour, whisking them in too, then stir in the chopped pistachio nuts. Put a spoonful of the mix on a silicone baking mat; spread it out until it is just slightly larger in diameter than the cut poached pear. Repeat to give eight tuiles, spacing them about 5cm apart. Bake until just golden. Allow to cool on the mat and keep them in an airtight container if preparing beforehand.

Finally, make the caramel sauce. As for the ice cream, cook the sugar to a caramel. Then add the cream and stir until dissolved.

To serve, place a ring in the centre of each serving plate as a guide and spoon the pear compote on the bottom. Remove the ring. Place the cooked pear on the centre of the compote, and carefully fill the space where the core was with caramel sauce. Cover the pear with a pistachio tuile and place a scoop of ice cream over it. Drizzle some caramel sauce over, and place the top of the pear on the side.

William Curley

Chocolatier, William Curley Richmond

Dark chocolate entremet
centred with a Maldon sea salt caramel

First, make the ice cream. Boil the milk. Once boiled, pour it into a container with the lemon thyme and allow it to infuse overnight. Split and scrape the seeds out of the vanilla pod. Sieve the milk into a pan and add the whipping cream, vanilla and 100g of the caster sugar. Whisk the egg yolks and the rest of the caster sugar together until light in colour. Prepare an ice-water bain-marie by putting a bowl in a container of water with lots of ice. Bring the milk and cream to the boil, then pour half the boiled milk and cream over the egg yolk mixture and whisk it. Put it back in the pan. Over a gentle heat, and with continuous stirring, cook the mixture to 85°C. Take the pan off the heat and pass the liquid through a fine sieve into the bowl sitting in the iced water bain-marie. Once it has cooled, transfer to a container and leave it overnight in the fridge. The following day churn it in an ice-cream machine, according to the manufacturer's instructions.

Prepare the apricot compote. Put the apricot purée and vanilla pod in a pan and bring to the boil. Rain in the sugar and powdered pectin, and cook it down. Then add the chopped apricots and allow to cool.

Next, make the sponge. Preheat the oven to 180°C/350°F/gas 4. Sift the flour and cocoa powder together. In a large mixing bowl, whisk the egg whites. Gradually add the sugar and increase the speed until you reach the soft-peak meringue stage. Then whisk in the egg yolks. Fold in the sifted flour and cocoa powder. Spread the mixture onto a 25cm x 30cm tray lined with a non-stick baking mat, and bake in the preheated oven for 18–20 minutes, or until the top of the sponge springs back when pressed. Allow to cool.

The next element of the dessert is the Maldon salt caramel. Boil the cream and vanilla pod together, then take off the heat and allow to infuse for 1 hour. Put the sugar and glucose in a heavy-based pan over a medium heat, and stir until they begin to melt. Then stop stirring and cook until the melted sugars turn to amber caramel. Strain the cream and bring it to the boil once more. Gradually add the warm cream to the caramel, mix it well and remove from the stove. Add the butter piece by piece, before finally adding the Maldon salt. Combine them well and allow to cool. Once cool, transfer to an airtight container until you are ready to assemble the dessert.

Continued on page 150…

Ingredients

You will need 12 moulds, ideally small rectangular ones, about 5cm deep, 10cm long and 4cm wide. If you don't have these then 175ml pudding moulds will work too.

For the lemon thyme ice cream:
1 litre milk
2 tbsp lemon thyme leaves
1 vanilla pod
250ml whipping cream
250g caster sugar
15 large egg yolks (or 275g in weight)

For the apricot compote:
250g apricot purée
half a vanilla pod
35g sugar
7.5g pectin powder (or 1½ tsp)
500g apricot halves, chopped

For the chocolate sponge:
75g flour
1 tbsp cocoa powder
2 medium egg whites (90g in weight)
90g caster sugar
7 medium egg yolks (110g in weight)

For the Maldon sea salt caramel:
320ml whipping cream
half a vanilla pod
500g sugar
80g glucose
400g butter, cubed
a pinch of Maldon sea salt

William Curley

Chocolatier, William Curley Richmond

Dark chocolate entremet *Continued*

For the dark chocolate glaze:
75g cocoa powder
14g gelatine
175ml water
225g caster sugar
125ml whipping cream

For the chocolate mousse:
320g chocolate, 70% cocoa solids
250ml milk
4 medium egg yolks (60g in weight)
45g caster sugar
450ml whipping cream

Serves 12

Prepare the dark chocolate glaze. Sieve the cocoa powder. Soak the gelatine in cold water; once it is soft, carefully strain off the excess water and discard it. Boil the 175ml water and the caster sugar together. Continue to boil on a low heat for 2–3 minutes, then add the sieved cocoa powder and the whipping cream. Return to the boil and simmer for 4–5 minutes. Remove the pan from the heat and add the soaked gelatine; mix it in. Pass the mixture through a fine sieve into a bowl and allow it to cool. Store in the fridge until needed.

The last thing to make is the chocolate mousse, as it needs to be used immediately. Finely chop the chocolate and put it in a mixing bowl. Pour the milk into a pan and bring it to the boil. While it is heating up, whisk together the egg yolks and sugar until the mixture becomes light in colour. When the milk has boiled, pour half onto the egg yolks and sugar mixture and mix thoroughly. Pour everything back into the pan and cook on a low heat, stirring continuously until the mixture reaches 82–84°C. Take the pan off the heat and pour the mixture through a fine sieve onto the chocolate. Using a spatula, combine until the mixture becomes smooth and emulsified, then leave it to cool. Put the cream into a bowl and whisk until soft peaks form, then carefully fold it into the cooled chocolate mixture.

It is now time to assemble the dessert. Cut the sponge into rectangles that will fit into your moulds; you will need two per mould. Have them handy.

Line the moulds with the freshly made mousse, ensuring there are no air bubbles. Place a layer of sponge in the mould. Pipe a generous amount of caramel on top, then top that with another layer of sponge. Fill the mould with more mousse, scrape it flat and freeze.

Once the desserts are completely frozen, unmould them carefully and put them on a wire rack. Slightly warm the glaze and pour it over the top of the unmoulded desserts, coating the top and sides evenly. Shake off any excess glaze by tapping the tray gently on the table. Place them on the serving plates and allow to defrost. Serve with apricot compote and lemon thyme ice cream.

Making ice cream without a machine

Not everyone has an ice-cream machine. Fortunately it is perfectly possible to make ice cream without one. The principles are the same whatever the flavourings.

Make the ice cream mixture as specified in the recipe. Put it into a large bowl, chilled over ice, and let it cool down. Once the ice-cream mixture is cold put the bowl into the freezer.

The ice cream should be beginning to set after about 30 minutes. Take the bowl out of the freezer and beat the ice-cream mixture with an electric whisk or a hand blender (be careful if your ice cream contains ingredients that you do not wish to pulverise – it can be done by hand), which breaks up the ice crystals. Then put the bowl back in the freezer. Repeat two or three times and then leave the ice cream to set until firm.

Tip: It is easier to use a whisk if you freeze the mixture in a bowl rather than a freezer box, but it can also be decanted into a food processor and then replaced in the box for refreezing.

Paul Gayler

Executive Chef, The Lanesborough

My chocolate brownies
with Maldon sea salt milk jam

Here is my recipe for the best chocolate brownies you will ever eat, enriched with a salted milk jam topping made from caramelised milk and honey. The addition of the Maldon salt is important as it gives the brownies a salty caramel flavour that is just wonderful. If you want to enjoy them, make plenty – they go pretty quickly in my home. A real teatime – anytime – treat!

Make the milk jam first. Bring the milk, honey, Maldon salt and sugar to the boil in a heavy-based pan, stirring all the time. Reduce to a low heat and cook it for one hour, stirring it often; be careful that it doesn't boil over or stick. The mixture should be very thick and reduced while having a lovely caramel colour. Put it into a bowl, leave it to go cold then cover and refrigerate until the next day.

Now for the brownies. Preheat the oven to 180°C/350°F/gas 4. Break up the chocolate into chunks. Put these pieces into a bowl with the butter and place it over a pan of simmering water (the bottom of the bowl must be clear of the surface of the water). Stir until the mixture is completely melted and smooth. Remove from the heat and allow it to cool a little. In another bowl, whip the eggs and sugar until fluffy, then carefully pour in the melted chocolate. Fold in the flour, baking powder and cocoa powder. Add the nuts; mix well until smooth and silky in consistency.

Line two 23cm square cake tins with greaseproof paper (allow the paper to overhang on two sides) and pour in the brownie mix, spreading it evenly. Place the tins in the oven for 25 minutes. Do not overcook them – brownies stiffen after cooking and the centres should be gooey, the outer edges slightly crisper and springy when you take them out of the oven.

Put the tins on a cooling rack and allow the brownies to cool thoroughly in the tins. Then carefully remove them from the tins, using the overhanging paper. Cut into squares, top each square with a smear of the prepared milk jam – and enjoy.

Ingredients

For the brownies:
275g dark chocolate
  (ideally 70% cocoa solids)
275g unsalted butter
3 free-range eggs
225g sugar
75g plain flour
½ tsp baking powder
30g cocoa powder
100g chopped hazelnuts or pecans

For the jam:
600ml full-fat milk
1 tbsp runny honey
a good pinch of Maldon sea salt
300g sugar

Makes 32 pieces

Gary Hunter

Head of Culinary Arts, Westminster Kingsway College

Bramley apple and lemon thyme crumble *with mascarpone ice cream and Maldon salted caramel sauce*

Ingredients

You will need 4 x 6cm stainless steel rings

For the crumble:
50g caster sugar
60g soft unsalted butter
55g ground almonds
½ tsp Maldon sea salt
60g soft white flour
3 Bramley apples
5 tsp clear thyme honey
25g unsalted butter
1 sprig fresh lemon thyme
10g sultanas

For the salted caramel sauce:
4 tbsp water
60g granulated sugar
6 tbsp double cream
a pinch Maldon sea salt

For the mascarpone ice cream:
250ml full-fat milk
150g mascarpone
3 egg yolks
75g caster sugar

Serves 4

Make the ice cream beforehand. Put the milk and half the mascarpone into a saucepan and bring to the boil. Beat together the egg yolks and caster sugar in a bowl, then add the milk mixture to the bowl and mix them together well. Return the ice-cream mixture to the saucepan and cook it until it reaches 85°C, stirring continuously. Put an empty bowl into a baking tray and fill the tray with iced water. Pass the mixture through a fine sieve into the bowl and allow it to chill. Stir in the remaining mascarpone and then freeze the mix in an ice-cream machine, following the manufacturer's instructions. Set aside in the freezer for later use.

Make the crumble. Preheat the oven to 180°C/350°F/gas 4, and mix the sugar with the butter, rubbing them together. Add the ground almonds, Maldon salt and flour and continue to rub everything together to create a crumbly texture. Spread the mixture onto a baking sheet lined with a silicone baking mat and bake for 15 minutes or until golden brown in colour. Remove from the oven and set aside.

Wash, peel and cut the Bramley apples into 1cm dice. In a shallow pan cook the honey, butter and lemon thyme until they reach a light caramel. Add the sultanas and then add the apples. Reduce the heat, place a piece of baking paper over the top and continue to cook slowly until the apples are soft to the touch but still maintain their shape. Remove from the heat.

Place four 6cm stainless steel rings on a silicone baking mat or baking sheet. Spoon a little of the crumble mix into the base of each ring and place on top enough of the cooked apple mixture to come two-thirds up the ring. Then put more crumble on top of the apples and place them in the oven for 12 minutes to warm through and further colour the crumble.

While the crumbles are cooking, make the sauce. Put the water and sugar in a heavy-based saucepan and cook them to a caramel. Mix the double cream and Maldon salt together and, off the heat, add them to the caramel carefully – it will rise up and spit. Return the pan to the heat and bring to the boil. Pass the sauce through a fine sieve. Set aside and keep warm.

Carefully lift each crumble onto its serving plate and remove the ring. Spoon the salted caramel sauce around it and set a quenelle of the ice cream to the side.

Regis Negrier

Head Pastry Chef, The Delaunay

Pot de crème au chocolat

The pot de crème au chocolat is a very classic and simple French dessert, and the salted caramel gives it a modern twist.

Make the salted caramel first. Put the sugar in a heavy-based pan over a moderate heat, stirring until it begins to melt. Stop stirring and cook until the sugar has turned to a dark caramel.

Remove the pan from the heat and add the two types of cream, stirring constantly with a whisk – stand back, because it will foam up and can spit. Add the butter and mix until it has melted (return it to a low heat if necessary). Sprinkle the Maldon salt over the caramel, stirring until it is dissolved, then remove the pan from the heat if you have replaced it there, and empty the caramel into a bowl. Set it to one side.

Then make the chocolate mixture. Cream the egg yolks and sugar together until the mixture forms a ribbon, and bring the cream and milk to the boil. Pour the boiling liquid on top of the egg mixture, whisking continuously. Then pour the mixture back into the pan and cook it over a low heat until it has thickened and the temperature has reached between 80–85°C.

Put the chopped chocolate in a bowl and pour the egg and cream mixture onto it, stirring all the while. If you have a hand blender, blend so that the mixture is smooth and emulsified; if not, beat it well. Divide the chocolate filling between the serving dishes – ramekins or glasses, perhaps – and put them in the fridge for an hour. Then pipe the salted caramel on top of the chocolate cream. Keep them refrigerated until you are ready to serve and, if you wish, top with some warm chocolate sauce before serving.

Ingredients

For the salted caramel:
150g sugar
50g whipping cream
50g double cream
60g butter
a pinch of Maldon sea salt

For the chocolate cream:
4 large egg yolks, or 90g pasteurised egg yolk
45g sugar
225g whipping cream
225ml milk
180g dark chocolate, 70% cocoa solids, finely chopped

Chocolate sauce for serving (optional)

Serves 8–10

Allan Picket

Head Chef, Plateau Restaurant

Rice pudding

Rice pudding is an absolute favourite with my children. The older boys love it with strawberry jam, but I think it works really well with compotes of any flavour (Bonne Maman do a good range). Adding a pinch of Maldon sea salt intensifies the flavours of the rice and other ingredients.

Ingredients

250ml double cream
750ml whole milk
125g caster sugar
half a vanilla pod
125g pudding rice
a pinch of Maldon sea salt

Serves 4, generously

Put the cream, milk and sugar in a large pan. Add the vanilla pod and bring to the boil. Pour in the rice slowly, stirring all the time, and add a pinch of Maldon salt.

The rice pudding can be cooked on top of the hob – lower the heat and simmer it for 2 hours, stirring so the rice doesn't catch – or in the oven. To do this, preheat the oven to 150°C/300°F/gas 2. Pour the rice into a greased baking dish, remove the vanilla pod (this can be removed before serving if you cook the pudding on the hob) and bake in the oven until tender.

Serve with either good quality jam or home-made fruit compote. Rice pudding works really well with cooked Bramley apples that have had a little cinnamon and a touch of sugar added to take the edge off them, and at Plateau we serve it with poached prunes. These are easy to do – just poach the prunes gently in weak Earl Grey tea (black, of course) with a little added orange zest.

Claire Clarke
The Carriage House

Rich chocolate ganache tart
with Maldon salted caramel and candied peanuts

I've chosen this recipe because not only does it display the versatility of Maldon salt brilliantly, it also holds special memories of my time working at the French Laundry in California. I was asked to make this recipe for the 'Michelin Man' who dined at the French Laundry during the time the Guide visited San Francisco in 2006.

If you are making the pastry in a food processor, place all the ingredients in the machine and pulse gently until they form a soft but not sticky dough. Alternatively, if making by hand, lightly cream the butter and sugar together with a wooden or plastic spoon. Beat the egg and add half to the creamed mixture a little at a time, beating well between each addition. Sift the flour and salt into a bowl or onto a piece of baking parchment and add to the creamed mixture all in one go. Bring the paste together gently to form a soft but not sticky dough, but do not overhandle it. Wrap the dough in cling film and chill for about 2 hours.

Lightly grease a 20cm loose-bottomed tart tin, and lightly flour a work surface. Roll the pastry out to about 5mm thick, and carefully line the tin with the pastry. Trim off the excess and leave the lined tart tin to rest in the fridge for 30 minutes.

Preheat the oven to 170°C/325°F/gas 3. Line the pastry case with cling film and fill it with baking beans. Bake it in the centre of the oven for 15–20 minutes, until the pastry has started to colour and the base is firm to touch; it should not be wet at this stage. Remove the package of beans and return the pastry case to the oven for about 10 minutes, until the pastry is golden brown. Leave it to cool completely.

Make the butterscotch sauce. Put the sugar and water in a small heavy-based pan and mix them well to dissolve the sugar. Bring to the boil, then boil over a high heat, without stirring, until the mixture develops a golden caramel colour. While it is boiling, clean the sides of the pan 4 or 5 times with a clean pastry brush dipped in cold water, running the brush around the edges of the pan to keep it free from sugar crystals that might fall back into the sugar and cause the caramel to crystallise.

Continued on page 162…

Ingredients

For the sweet pastry:
70g softened unsalted butter
50g caster sugar
1 small egg, beaten (use half)
125g plain flour
a small pinch of Maldon sea salt

For the butterscotch sauce:
125g caster sugar
4 tbsp water
125ml double cream
1 tbsp rum

For the tart:
2 tbsp butterscotch sauce
2 tsp Maldon sea salt
225ml double cream
180g chocolate, 70% cocoa solids, finely chopped
45g chocolate, 72% cocoa solids, finely chopped

For the candied peanuts:
60g caster sugar
4 tbsp water
75g shelled unsalted peanuts
250ml canola or vegetable oil for frying

Serves 6

Claire Clarke

The Carriage House

Rich chocolate ganache tart *Continued*

While the sugar is cooking, bring the cream to the boil in a separate pan. Once the syrup turns a golden caramel colour, remove it from the heat and leave it for a few more seconds to colour up more; it will do this naturally as it cools. As soon as it reaches a dark caramel, gradually add the hot cream. Do this very slowly, adding a little at a time, as the sugar will still be very hot and will spit and bubble up. Once all the cream has been added, return the pan to the heat and whisk gently until it boils and all the sugar has been dissolved. Stir in the rum, pour the sauce into a clean bowl or jug and leave it to cool completely.

Now fill the tart. Mix 2 tablespoons of the butterscotch sauce with a teaspoon of Maldon salt (the other teaspoon will be scattered over the top at the end) and spread it over the base of the pastry case. Put the tart tin on a baking sheet.

To make the tart filling, bring 150ml of the cream to the boil. Place the remaining cream in a large mixing bowl with all the finely chopped chocolate. Pour the boiled cream over the chocolate and leave for 30 seconds, then whisk very gently – this is important – to make a smooth shiny ganache. Do not whisk energetically or your ganache will have too many air bubbles, which will spoil the surface of the tart. Pour the ganache immediately into the centre of the pastry case and level it by shaking the baking sheet. Do not use a spatula or palette knife to do this, as that would dull the shiny surface. Leave the tart to set and firm up at room temperature. Do not refrigerate.

To make the candied peanuts, put the sugar and water in a pan and bring to the boil, stirring to dissolve the sugar. Add the peanuts and simmer for 10–15 minutes, until the sugar syrup thickens a little. Meanwhile, heat the oil in a deep pan to 180°C. Using a slotted spoon, remove the peanuts from the syrup and drop them in the hot oil. Cook for 4–5 minutes or until golden brown, then drain them on kitchen paper, transfer to a piece of foil or large sieve and allow them to cool. While they are cooling, use a fork to separate any that have stuck together. Once they are completely cold, sprinkle them over the top of the tart with the remaining teaspoon of Maldon salt. Serve with crème fraiche or Greek yoghurt.

Daniel Richardson

Head Chef, Hartwell House Hotel

Goat's curd parfait
with Maldon salted pistachio ice cream and a spiced biscuit

Make the goat's curd parfait first. You will need either 6 x 100ml moulds, or 6 larger ones (175ml is a common size) which will only be partly filled. Whisk the egg yolk and 1 small teaspoon of the sugar together until you have a light froth. Boil a tablespoon of milk and 2 tablespoons of sugar together until they reach the thread stage, testing it on a very cold saucer (110°C; work quickly as it moves on to the soft-ball stage fairly fast), then remove the pan from the heat and pour the contents onto the frothy sabayon. Whisk until it is pale and thick.

In a separate bowl, whisk another small teaspoon of sugar and the egg white together until they form soft peaks. Put the rest of the sugar – it should be a tablespoon – in a pan with a tablespoon of water and bring them to the boil. This time you want to get it to the soft-ball stage, testing it on a cold saucer once more, and then pour it onto the egg whites to make an Italian meringue. Whisk, continuously, until the mixture is cold.

Melt the white chocolate in a bowl over a pan of simmering water. Semi-whip the cream (it should be no firmer than this – it should just hold a trail when you lift out the whisk) while the chocolate is melting, and whisk the goat's curd a little to break up any lumps. Take the bowl off the heat and allow the chocolate to cool down until it is warm rather than hot, then fold the warm melted chocolate into the sabayon. Fold in half the Italian meringue, followed by the goat's curd, which you can whisk in very gently. Then fold in the remaining meringue, followed by the semi-whipped cream. Pipe it into the individual moulds and freeze.

Then prepare the ice cream. Grind 60g of the pistachios as finely as possible. Set them aside and chop the rest. Pour the cream and milk into a heavy-bottomed saucepan and add the ground pistachios. Bring it to the boil slowly, and boil it for a minute. Then lower the heat and allow it to infuse for a couple of minutes more. Put the egg yolks and sugar in a bowl and beat until creamy and smooth; the whisk should just leave a ribbon-like trail when you lift it out. Pour the milk and cream mixture gradually and very carefully into the egg mixture, stirring all the while and taking care at the start, as that's when there is most danger of curdling. Return the mixture to the pan and cook it gently, stirring continuously, over a low heat until it thickens. Be very careful not to boil it.

Continued on page 165…

Ingredients

For the goat's curd parfait:
1 medium egg yolk
55g sugar
1 tbsp milk
30g egg whites, or the white of one medium egg
40g good-quality white chocolate
75ml double cream
125g goat's curds

For the salted pistachio ice cream:
100g peeled unsalted pistachios
250ml cream
250ml milk
6 egg yolks
125g sugar
a pinch of Maldon sea salt

For the spiced biscuit:
100g flour
½ tsp cinnamon
½ tsp baking powder
a pinch of Maldon sea salt
50g butter
65g soft brown sugar
1 small egg, beaten
2 tbsp milk

For the chocolate decoration:
75g dark chocolate, chopped
edible green glitter

Serves 6

Daniel Richardson

Head Chef, Hartwell House Hotel

Goat's curd parfait *Continued*

When the mixture coats the back of a spoon, take the pan off the heat and add the chopped pistachios and Maldon salt. Mix them in, and set the mixture to one side to cool. Chill, transfer to an ice-cream maker and churn, following the manufacturer's instructions.

Now for the biscuit dough, which is soft and needs to be kept in the freezer in order for it to be handled easily. Sieve the flour, cinnamon, baking powder and Maldon salt together. Cream the butter and sugar lightly in a food processor, then measure out a tablespoon of the egg and add it gradually, mixing it in gently on a low speed. Add the sieved ingredients and bring everything together, still on a low speed, and adding just enough milk to make a soft but not sticky dough.

Put some baking paper on a work surface, and put the dough on it. Flour your hands lightly and roll it gently into a sausage, then wrap it up in the paper. Twist the ends together to hold the roll securely and put it in the freezer for at least 30 minutes. Slice finely and freeze again (you can keep the slices of dough in a plastic container stacked between sheets of baking paper for ease of use). Preheat the oven to 180°C/350°F/gas 4. Line a baking tray with more greaseproof paper and place slices of biscuit dough on it, about 5cm apart. Bake them for 15–20 minutes, or until they are golden brown – the time will depend on how thickly you have sliced the dough. Take the tray out of the oven and let the biscuits rest for 1–2 minutes, gently separate them from the paper and put on a rack to cool.

Finally, prepare the chocolate decoration. Put two-thirds of the chocolate in a bowl over a pan of simmering water, and melt it slowly. Then remove the bowl from the pan and add the rest of the chocolate, stirring until it also melts. Put out a textured acetate sheet. Sprinkle the sheet with edible green glitter dust, then spread the tempered dark chocolate thinly over it. Cut it into whatever shapes you like just as it sets, but leave them on the sheet. Line a baking tray with parchment paper and store the chocolate pieces, still attached to the sheet, upside down. Put a second tray on top to keep the sheet flat.

When you are ready to serve, remove the parfaits from the freezer and demould one onto each dessert plate. Add a rocher or ball of the ice cream, garnish with the spiced biscuit and chocolate decoration, and serve immediately.

Tip: If you can find it, you can use 25g pistachio compound in the salted pistachio ice cream in place of 60g of the pistachios. Add the pistachio compound with the 40g of chopped pistachios.

Ben Purton

Executive Head Chef, The Royal Horseguards Hotel and One Whitehall Place

Maldon salted dark chocolate fondant *with Maldon salted caramel and macadamia ice cream*

This dessert should have a liquid centre, so I advise cooking a test fondant beforehand (and of course eating it!) so you can tell if you need to adjust the cooking times…

Just as with Maldon salt, I love to use only the best ingredients, so a fantastic dark couverture such as Araguani from Valrhona, or Felchlin's Bolivian Cru Sauvage or the Extra Bitter 70% Callabaut will really boost the cacao notes in this fondant recipe. If you are limited to a supermarket selection, then we recommend Green and Black's.

Ingredients

For the ice cream:
200ml pasteurised egg yolk
300g caster sugar
500ml double cream
500ml milk
1 vanilla pod, seeded
200g macadamia nuts
2 tsp Maldon sea salt

For the fondants:
250g dark chocolate couverture
  (minimum 60% cocoa solids)
250g unsalted butter
5 whole eggs
5 egg yolks
300g caster sugar
250g plain flour
2 tsp Maldon sea salt

Serves 8

Begin by making the ice cream. In a large bowl, mix the yolks and 200g of the sugar together thoroughly, so that there are no lumps. Do this in advance, and you will find the custard cooks quicker as the sugar draws moisture from the eggs. If you cannot get pasteurised egg yolk (see page 183) then just use the equivalent weight in separated egg yolks.

Boil the cream and milk with the vanilla pod – this will release the oils and aromatic flavours. Pour half the liquid over the yolk mix, and stir it with a whisk to incorporate it quickly. Return the pan to the hob, and then pour all the egg mix back into the milk remaining in the pan. Lower the heat and continue to stir with a spatula; raise the temperature gradually until it reaches 82°C or until it is thick and coats the back of a spoon. Be careful, as if you heat the mix too far the custard will curdle or split. As soon as the custard is cooked, remove it from the heat and pass it through a fine sieve into a bowl or container. Immediately chill it over ice to stop the cooking process.

Preheat the oven to 180°C/350°F/gas 4 and line a baking tray with greaseproof paper. Spread the macadamia nuts out on it and roast them in the oven while the custard is cooling. Take them out as soon as they are a rich golden brown.

Put the rest of the sugar into a clean, dry, heavy-based pan and, over a medium heat, begin to melt it down. Using a wooden spoon, move the sugar around as it melts and starts to colour. You will need to take this

Continued on page 168…

Ben Purton

Executive Head Chef, The Royal Horseguards Hotel and One Whitehall Place

Maldon salted dark chocolate fondant *Continued*

sugar to the caramel stage which is at least 180°C, so be very careful. When the colour is golden, and all the sugar crystals are melted and the syrup is clear, pour the caramel over the nuts and leave it to set. Once cool, break up the caramel, smashing it lightly with the end of a rolling pin to create smaller bite-sized chunks. Sprinkle the Maldon salt into the mix.

Place the custard in an ice-cream machine and churn until thick and almost frozen, following the manufacturer's instructions. Then fold in the caramel chunks and Maldon salt and place the ice cream in the freezer to set up and crystallise a little more. Make sure the ice cream is not too runny when you mix in the caramel as otherwise the salt may dissolve – it is a much tastier effect to have the flakes melt in the mouth.

Now for the fondants. Heat the oven to 200°C/400°F/gas 6.

Melt the chocolate and butter until smooth and lump free. The chocolate should not get too hot – it will be fully liquid at 30°C and burn above 60°C – and your mix should be warm, not hot. You can use a microwave if you can set a low enough power and melt it slowly; otherwise put it in a dry bowl over a pan of simmering water, with the bottom of the bowl clear of the surface of the water. Be careful not to get any water in the mix or it can seize.

Lightly whisk the eggs and sugar together. If you have melted the chocolate in a bowl over water, take the bowl off the pan. Stir the egg mixture into the melted chocolate, then fold in the flour and the Maldon salt.

Grease and sugar 8 large ramekins or grease and line 8 dessert rings. Pipe or spoon the mixture into these moulds until they are about three-quarters full. Just before serving, cook for about 8–12 minutes – depending on the size of the mould and thickness of the edges – until the mix has risen, but the cake should not be cooked all the way through.

Remove from the oven, and serve with the ice cream on the side.

Tip: If you are short on time, or don't have an ice-cream machine, just make the caramel nut mix and fold it into some shop-bought, high-quality vanilla ice cream… Shhhh, no one will know!

Caramel without tears

Salted caramels are very popular – and delicious – but making caramel can sometimes be problematic. Here are some tricks and tips to help.

- Firstly, and most importantly: be careful. Boiling sugar – the basis of all caramel – can cause nasty burns, and adding cream or other liquid to a caramel will make it spit. Stand well back, and use a long-handled wooden spoon. Using a larger pan than you think strictly necessary is often a good idea, because caramel will bubble up wildly once additions are made.

- There are two basic ways of making caramel; the wet and dry methods. The dry method is the one most frequently used in this book, but the wet method may be useful if you find the dry one problematic. For this, you need an amount of water which is equivalent to half the weight of sugar, so if the recipe specifies 200g of sugar, you need 100ml of water.

Put the water in a heavy-based pan over a low heat and sprinkle in the sugar. It will gradually dissolve; stir it occasionally as it does so. Once the sugar has completely dissolved, increase the heat to a brisk simmer. Continue simmering for about 15 minutes or until the syrup starts to change colour. Don't stir it during this time, but do swirl the pan gently. In another 5 minutes or so it should be a deep amber colour. Take it off the heat immediately and put it in a shallow ice-water bath to stop it from continuing to cook (the pan will hiss dramatically, but ignore it). The caramel is now ready to use.

Continued on page 170…

Caramel without tears *Continued*

- Making caramel with fine sugar is often easier as it dissolves quickly and smoothly, which is why caster sugar is often specified.

- It can be difficult to judge the colour changes of caramel in a pan with a dark or non-stick interior. If possible, try to use a heavy-based but light-coloured pan, such as one in enamel or stainless steel. Thinner pans heat unevenly, which won't help, so use a good heavyweight one. And don't worry about cleaning the pan afterwards, because ...

- ... it's easy to clean pans which have been used to cook caramel. Add water to the sticky pan, place it over a low heat – and the caramel will dissolve.

- You have to work quickly with caramel because it sets while you're thinking about it. However, gently reheating the pan will soften it up again.

- There shouldn't be any gritty sugar crystals in a well-made caramel. To avoid this, keep a wet pastry brush to hand and use it to wipe down the interior sides of the pan. Granules can form there and fall back into the caramel, or become incorporated when the caramel is poured out.

- Caramel can sometimes separate once other ingredients have been added. If it does, take the pan off the heat and add a tablespoon of very hot water. Stir vigorously to recombine before returning to the heat. (Don't add more than two or three spoonfuls, though.)

- Finally, be careful not to overcook caramel as the burnt taste is quite unpleasant, so keep an eye on it. If it does burn, there's no alternative – you have to start again.

Alan Coxon
Managing Director, Coxon's Kitchen

Milk puffs
with spiced syrup

Prepare the syrup. Put all the ingredients in a small pan over a medium heat and bring to a simmer, stirring continuously. Once the sugar has dissolved bring it to a rolling boil and cook it for about 10 minutes or until the mixture has reached a syrupy consistency. Then turn off the heat and leave the syrup to cool. Then strain it into a bowl through muslin or a fine sieve and set it aside while you make the puffs.

Sieve the milk powder, flour, salt and baking powder into a bowl and mix them together, then add the cardamom. Add the cream cheese and rub it in until it has a sandy, crumb-like texture. Add the egg and mix it into the crumb, then gradually add a little of the milk until you obtain a smooth dough that holds its shape and is slightly sticky to the touch. Leave it to rest for 4–5 minutes, then divide it and roll it into ten equal-sized balls.

Meanwhile, preheat the fat or oil for deep frying – it needs to be 180°C. Gently add the balls to the oil and deep-fry them for approximately 4 minutes until light and golden. When they are ready, lift them from the oil using a slotted spoon and place them on kitchen paper to absorb any excess fat. Put them into a bowl, coat with the syrup – and serve.

Ingredients

For the milk puffs:
90g milk powder
40g self-raising flour
¼ tsp Maldon sea salt
1 tsp baking powder
½ tsp crushed cardamom seeds
50g Philadelphia full-fat
    cream cheese
1 medium egg, whisked
2 tbsp milk
375g ghee (or oil), for deep frying

For the spiced syrup:
200g sugar
300ml water
1¼ tsp cardamom seeds, crushed
2 slices of fresh chilli
a pinch of ground cinnamon

Serves 2 (5 puffs each)

Yolande Stanley

Lecturer in Patisserie, Westminster Kingsway College

Maldon sea salt nut caramel tarts

I chose this simply because it tastes great, and anything with chocolate is a winner!

Make the paste first. Lightly cream together the butter, salt, icing sugar, seeds from the vanilla pod and lemon zest using a hand mixer. Add the beaten egg a little at a time, then fold in the flour. Knead the paste briefly, enough to get it to come together, and then divide it into 10 equal pieces. Press it into the individual tartlet moulds and chill in the fridge for 30 minutes. Preheat the oven to 190°C/375°F/gas 5. Bake the cases blind until golden and dry, which will take about 10 minutes. Remove from the oven and set aside to cool.

Make the salted nut and mango caramel next. Put the caster sugar and glucose in a heavy-based pan over a medium heat and stir until they begin to melt and caramelise. Then stop stirring and continue cooking until the caramel turns a much deeper, rich brown colour. Off the heat, carefully add the cream and then return the pan to the heat. Stir until the caramel has dissolved. Then add the mango purée, ginger, butter and Maldon salt and cook to 121°C (if the mixture separates, take the pan off the heat, add a tablespoon of very hot water and stir vigorously to recombine before replacing the pan on the hob). Then fold in the nuts, reserving a few to use as a garnish. Put the mixture aside to cool.

When you are almost ready to serve, make the ganache; it is best if used immediately. Put the chopped chocolate in a bowl. Boil the cream and glucose together, and then pour onto the chocolate. Stir well to emulsify, and then add the butter, and stir that in too.

Take the tartlet tins out of the fridge. Spoon in some nutty caramel to come halfway up the tartlet, then transfer the ganache to a piping bag and top the caramel with a large blob of the chocolate (you can use a spoon if necessary, and can also refrigerate them for a short while). Top each tart with a peanut and a walnut piece before serving, and add an optional disc of tempered chocolate.

Ingredients

For the sable paste:
150g butter
½ tsp Maldon sea salt
75g icing sugar
half a vanilla pod – seeds only
zest of half a lemon, finely grated
1 medium egg, beaten
250g plain flour

For the nut caramel:
125g caster sugar
125g glucose
150ml whipping cream, warmed
125g mango purée
a small pinch of dried ginger
100g butter
1 tsp Maldon sea salt
50g unsalted roasted peanuts
50g walnuts, broken

For the ganache:
200g dark chocolate couverture
   (ideally 58–60% cocoa solids),
   finely chopped
150ml whipping cream
20g glucose
40g unsalted butter

You will need 10 12cm tartlet tins.

Serves 10

David Simms

Co-Founder and Director of Kendall and Simms

Apple and anise tarte Tatin
with caramel and Maldon sea salt ice cream

Ingredients

For the tarte Tatin:
240g caster sugar
120g butter, diced
4 large Braeburn apples
8 whole star anise
500g all-butter puff pastry sheet,
rolled thinly – to about 3mm thick

8 individual moulds
    10cm wide x 4cm high

For the ice cream:
750ml milk
250g caster sugar
250ml double cream
10 egg yolks
1 tsp Maldon sea salt

Serves 8

Make the ice cream first; it will keep in the freezer for a month anyway. Combine milk and cream in a heavy-based pan and bring to the boil. In a large bowl, mix the egg yolks with 100g of the sugar.

Put the rest of the sugar in a dry heavy-based pan over a moderate heat to make caramel. Stir it until it begins to melt, then stop stirring and continue cooking until the sugar deepens in colour. Then remove the pan from the heat and carefully pour in the milk and cream. Return the pan to the heat until the caramel has dissolved. Take the pan off the heat, allow it to cool a little and then pour it over the egg mixture. Mix. Pour everything back into the pan and cook it on a low heat, stirring continuously, until it reaches 84°C; do not let it boil. Then pass it through a fine sieve, add the Maldon salt and set it aside to chill overnight. The next day, churn it in an ice-cream machine and use as required.

For the tarte Tatin begin by making a light caramel with the sugar in a dry heavy-bottomed pan, in the same way as for the ice cream. When it is a light amber colour, pull the pan off the heat and whisk in the diced butter. Divide the caramel between the moulds and allow it to set.

Peel and core the apples. Then cut each one in half widthways. Stud the flat side of each half with one whole star anise, putting it where the core was. Roll out the puff pastry thinly on a floured surface, and cut out discs of the pastry (they should be big enough to encase the apples and about the same size as the moulds). Put the flat side of the apple on the table and mould the pastry over the top of the apple ensuring it meets the edges . Prick the pastry all over with a fork and then place one into each mould.

Preheat the oven to 150°C/300°F/gas 2. Place the moulds on baking sheets and cook for 30–45 minutes, until golden. Remove from the oven, allow to cool for 3–4 minutes, then turn out carefully and serve with the caramel and Maldon salt ice cream.

Richard Tonks
Executive Chef, Brooks's

Black Velvet trinity burnt cream

Brooks's Club doors have been opened to its members since 1764. In 1861, Black Velvet, a champagne and Guinness cocktail, was created by Brooks's barman to mourn the death of Prince Albert, Queen Victoria's Prince Consort. The Club held a dinner in December 2011 to commemorate the 150th anniversary of his death and, in preparation for the event, developed this dessert.

Preheat the oven to 140°C/275°F/gas 1. Split the vanilla pod and scrape out the dark seeds with a sharp knife. Put the cream, milk and the vanilla pod into a saucepan and heat the liquid to boiling point. Remove the pan from the heat, cover it with a lid, and leave to infuse for 10 minutes.

Discard the vanilla pod. Mix the Guinness, champagne and orange zest together, and then add the mixture to the infused boiled milk. Whisk the egg yolks with 50g of the sugar until pale and thick, then add the cream and the Guinness mixture. Stir it well, then pour the liquid into 250ml ramekins.

Place the ramekins in a baking dish or roasting tin and put hand-hot water into the dish so that it comes about halfway up the sides of the ramekins. Put the dish into the oven and cook the cream until just set, which will take approximately 30–35 minutes. Allow to cool, and then place the ramekins in the fridge for a few hours.

When you are ready to serve, evenly sprinkle the tops of the ramekins with caster sugar. Using a blow torch, caramelise the tops. Put the ramekins on the serving plates and decorate with the madeleines, blackberries, raspberries, sprigs of mint and dust lightly with icing sugar. Serve with a scoop of the ice cream with a pinch of Maldon salt to the side.

Ingredients

250ml double cream
75ml full-fat milk
1 vanilla pod
8 egg yolks
zest of 1 orange
50g caster sugar
275ml Guinness
50ml Champagne

For the topping and presentation:
3–4 tbsp caster sugar
10 madeleines
10 blackberries
5 raspberries
5 sprigs of mint
icing sugar for dusting

To serve:
A scoop of good quality vanilla ice cream and a pinch of Maldon sea salt per person

Serves 5

Sara Jayne Stanes
CEO, The Academy of Culinary Arts

Chocolate truffles
with Maldon sea salt

Chocolate truffles are rich, infatuating little follies, named because – when dusted with cocoa powder – they resemble those rare earthy little gems of fungus; they are similarly precious to all lovers of exciting food. I am a fan of the very lightly whisked variety, with its resulting lightness. Maldon salt brings out the spiciness of the chocolate and balances the sweetness – delicious!

Ingredients

Makes about 40–45

225g very best quality chocolate
300ml double or whipping cream
¼ tsp Maldon sea salt, crushed

Your choice of rolling materials:
cocoa powder, icing sugar, finely
chopped nuts...

Break or chop the chocolate into evenly sized small pieces, the size of buttons, and put it in a large mixing bowl, at least 1.75 litres in size. Put a saucepan over a medium heat, add the cream and bring it to a rolling boil. Add the Maldon salt, stir, and immediately pour the hot cream over the chocolate. Stir well, blending thoroughly until all the chocolate is melted. Leave the mixture to cool at room temperature, which will take at least 1–1½ hours.

Then you can proceed to making the truffles. This is the method I use, and I think by far the most satisfactory for creating a light airy truffle. Take a large, heavy chopping board or a baking tray and cover it tightly and completely with cling film or waxed paper (you may need to fix it with sticky tape underneath to make sure it is taut – if you don't wrap the film tightly enough, it lifts up when you try to remove the truffles when they are set).

Using an electric hand whisk, gently whisk the mixture to the point where it just begins to stop 'running' – the mixture should just begin to thicken, and the whisk barely leave a trail when you lift it from the mixture. Stop whisking while it is still soft, otherwise it might separate. Then transfer the mixture into a 35cm piping bag with a 1cm nozzle and pipe little truffle spheres onto the film-covered chopping board or baking sheet. Refrigerate for about an hour.

Alternatively, you can use a teaspoon to measure out little bite-size portions when the mixture has set in the bowl. Dust your hands with icing sugar to prevent the truffles from sticking and roll them into balls in the palms of your hands. This is very messy but just as good as the first method.

Finally, finish the truffles by rolling them in your coating of choice – good-quality cocoa powder, icing sugar, chopped nuts, chocolate vermicelli... The truffles will keep for at least a week, and you can always sprinkle them with cocoa powder from a sieve or tea strainer at the last minute if they need 'tarting up'.

Alain Roux

Chef Patron, The Waterside Inn

Soft chocolate caramel
with almonds and Maldon sea salt

Preheat the oven to 180°C/350°F/gas 4; butter and line a 23cm square tin with greaseproof paper.

Chop the almonds roughly, then spread them on a baking sheet and put them in the oven until they are light brown in colour. Remove the tray from the oven and allow to cool. Crush the Maldon salt with a rolling pin and mix it with the butter.

Put the double cream, caster sugar and glucose in a heavy-based pan. Bring it to the boil gradually, stirring just a little as the sugar and glucose dissolve. The mixture needs to reach 121°C – while it is coming up to this temperature, stir it gently with the thermometer (which helps to prevent caramel sticking to the bulb and distorting the reading), and when the thermometer is within 10–15 degrees of the desired heat, lower the heat a little to prevent overheating. Take it off the heat immediately and add the almonds, the chocolate and the salted butter mix. Stir everything together thoroughly until the chocolate and butter have melted completely, then pour the caramel into the tin.

Place a sheet of greaseproof paper on the top and leave it to cool down completely. Cut it into squares with a large knife and store in an airtight container.

Tip: If the caramel is too soft, cook it to 1 or 2 degrees more. If it is too hard for your taste, decrease the cooking by 1 or 2 degrees next time.

Ingredients

Makes 1 x 23cm square tin; approximately 20 pieces

175g whole blanched almonds
a pinch of Maldon sea salt
10g butter
150ml double cream
175g caster sugar
75g glucose
100g dark bitter chocolate, finely chopped

Andrew Turner

Executive Head Chef, The Café Royal

Boule de Café

Ingredients

100ml cream
100g sugar
4 tbsp golden syrup
50g butter
Maldon sea salt, to taste
30 dark chocolate shells
100g dark chocolate, 55% cocoa
  solids
200g feuillentine paillete
  (alternatively, use finely crushed
  Coco Pops)

Put the cream in a pan and bring it to the boil over a medium heat; allow it to cool slightly. Put another large pan on the stove, also over a medium heat, and add the sugar gradually, stirring until it is just golden brown. Then add the golden syrup, again gradually, before slowly adding the warm cream; it will bubble up, so be careful. Remove from the heat and stir in the butter, and add Maldon salt to taste. Leave the mixture until it is cool.

Put the chocolate shells out on a baking tray; if they are completely spherical, rest them in small paper cases or give each one a spot of caramel to sit on so it will not roll around. Pipe the filling into them until it comes up to just under the brim (you can use a small jug as an alternative). Then carefully transfer the tray to the fridge and leave them until set.

Take the tray out of the fridge. Melt the chocolate in a bowl over a pan of hot water and then allow it to cool a little before pouring it into the openings to seal the chocolate balls. Return the tray to the fridge to allow the chocolate to set. Once everything is set, roll the balls in the feuillentine until completely covered. Replace the tray in the fridge until you are ready to serve. Sprinkle a little Maldon salt on top of each one before serving.

Unusual ingredients

Most of the ingredients can be obtained comparatively easily. Large supermarkets often carry a surprising range of (sometimes specialist) ingredients, and oriental and Indian supermarkets are an excellent resource, as are farmers' markets. Liquid and powdered glucose can be found in good chemists, and in some health food shops. Failing access to these, there is always the internet.

The following site addresses were correct at the time of publication:

- Champagne vinegar: www.melburyandappleton.co.uk
- Chocolate couverture: try www.choc-o-holic.co.uk or www.chocolate.co.uk
- Goat's curd: www.pantmawrcheeses.co.uk
- Gull's eggs: www.finefoodspecialist.co.uk
- Dark chocolate balls: www.callebaut.com or www.chocolatetradingco.com
- Fennel pollen: www.gourmelli.co.uk
- Megrim sole: www.thecornishfishmonger.co.uk
- Mooli: Indian supermarkets, or try www.ennerdalesgreengrocers.co.uk
- Panko breadcrumbs: large supermarkets, or try www.japanesekitchen.co.uk
- Pasteurised egg yolks, widely used in restaurants: www.allanreederltd.co.uk
- Pectin: try larger supermarkets, often in with jam-making ingredients, sugar, etc.
- Pistachio compound: try retailers of materials for professional cake-making, or specialists such as www.msk-ingredients.com
- Sea vegetables: www.westlandswow.co.uk/taste-of-the-sea.php
- Szechuan peppercorns: large supermarkets or online retailers such as www.theasiancookshop.co.uk
- Textured acetate sheet and other chocolate decorations: www.thecakedecoratingcompany.co.uk. Lakeland also carries a good range of baking supplies: www.lakeland.co.uk
- Trompette de Mort mushrooms: www.finefoodspecialist.co.uk
- Truffle juice: www.finefoodspecialist.co.uk

Online specialist supermarkets, such as www.wingyip.com or www.itadka.com

Acknowledgements

First and foremost, we would like to thank everyone from the Academy of Culinary Arts, for their committed outreach to members and valuable contribution to **Desert Island Dishes**. In particular, we wish to thank Chairman John Williams, President Brian Turner, Chief Executive Sara Jayne Stanes and Sara's personal assistant Consola Evans for their constant efforts, communications and overwhelming support. We would also like to thank Brian for writing the book's foreword.

Our thanks also go to Jay Rayner, award-winning British journalist, writer, broadcaster and food critic, who wrote the book's main introduction. Additionally, Jay took the time to visit the Maldon Salt Company to gain a real insight into its work. We really appreciate this as Jay was then able to communicate the true Maldon story.

The food photography in this book has really brought **Desert Island Dishes** to life. Therefore we would like to say thank you to photographer Tony Briscoe, food stylist Penny Stephens and prop stylist Rebecca Williams for all of their outstanding work.

We would also like to thank Kate Santon, who tested and edited the recipes and Darren Hayball, who worked hard to achieve the book's design.

We would like to show our appreciation to Cool Cucumber TV who have been significantly active in the book's online presence, producing online video and blogger content with a selection of Academy chefs.

Finally, without the contributions from the following Academy of Culinary Arts chefs, **Desert Island Dishes** would not have been possible. Therefore, a huge thank you goes to:

Adam Byatt, Chef Proprietor, Trinity Restaurant

Alain Roux, Chef Patron, The Waterside Inn

Alan Coxon, Managing Director, Coxon's Kitchen

Albert Roux, Maître Cuisinier de France

Allan Picket, Head Chef, Plateau Restaurant

Lawrence Keogh, Head Chef, The Wolseley

Regis Negrier, Head Pastry Chef, The Delaunay

Andrew Turner, Executive Head Chef, The Café Royal

Richard Tonks, Executive Chef, Brooks

Yolande Stanley, Lecturer in Patisserie, Westminster Kingsway College

David Simms, Co-founder and Director of Kendall and Simms

Daniel Richardson, Head Chef, Hartwell House Hotel

Ben Purton, Executive Head Chef, The Royal Horseguards Hotel and One Whitehall Place

Gary Hunter, Head of Culinary Arts, Westminster Kingsway College

Paul Gayler, Executive Chef, the Lanesborough

William Curley, Chocolatier, William Curley Richmond

Claire Clarke, The Carriage House

Benoit Blin, Head Pastry Chef, Le Manoir aux Quat'Saisons

John Williams, Executive Chef, The Ritz London

Nick Vadis, UK Executive Chef, Compass Group UK & Ireland

David Sharland, Executive Chef, The Seafood Restaurant

Brian Turner CBE, President of The Academy of Culinary Arts

Rick Stein, Chef Proprietor, The Seafood Restaurant

Gary Rhodes, Restaurant Associates UK, Fourth Floor

Martyn Nail, Executive Chef, Claridges

Herbert Berger

Paul Heathcote, Proprietor, PH Restaurants Ltd

Peter Fiori, Executive Chef, Coutts Bank

Mark Dodson, Chef Proprietor, The Mason's Arms

Jim Cowie, Chef Patron, Captain's Galley Seafood Restaurant

Philip Corrick, Executive Chef of Clubhouses, Royal Automobile Club

Prof. Peter A. Jones MBE, Director of Wentworth Jones, tourism and hospitality specialists

Kevin Cape, Executive Chef, Shook Restaurant

Billy Campbell, Executive Chef, Thistle Glasgow

Tony Cameron, Chef de Cuisine, The Oriental Club

Jason Atherton, Chef Patron, Pollen Street Social

Neil Thrift, Head Chef, Waldorf Astoria

Frances Bissell, Consultant Chef and food writer

Richard Shepherd, Chef Patron, Coq d'Or Restaurant Company Ltd

Dereck Quelch, Executive Chef, The Goring

David Pitchford, Head Chef, Reads Restaurant with Rooms

Luke Matthews, Executive Chef, Chewton Glen

Rob Kirby, Chef Director, Lexington

André Garrett MCA, Head Chef, Galvin at Windows

Chris and Jeff Galvin, Chef Patrons, Galvin Restaurants

Simon Fooks, Head Chef, Merchant Taylors Catering

Stephen Doherty, Chef Director, First Floor Café, Lakeland Ltd

Adam Byatt, Chef Proprietor, Trinity Restaurant

Stefano Borella, Group Pastry Chef/ lecturer in La Cucina Caldesi Cookery School Caldesi Restaurants Ltd

Paul Askew, Food and Beverage Director and Chef Patron, The London Carriage Works and Hope Street Hotel

Terry Tinton, Programme Manager, Senior Lecturer in Culinary Arts, Westminster Kingsway College

Recipe index

Note: Page numbers in *italics* denote photos of dishes

Chef index

Note: Page numbers in *italics* denote photos of dishes

Richard Tonks • Martyn Nail • Peter A. Jones • Alain
Sara Jane Stanes • Alan Coxon • Jim Cowie • Stef
Chris Galvin • Kevin Cape • Jeff Galvin • Regis Negrier • A
Terry Tinton • Derek Quelch • Mark Dodson • Paul Gayler
Allan Picket • Neil Thrift • Peter Fiori • Philip Corrick • Stephe
David Simms • Rob Kirby • Herbert Berger • John W
Tony Cameron • Daniel Richardson • Jason Atherton • Yolan
Richard Tonks • Martyn Nail • Peter A. Jones • Alain
Sara Jane Stanes • Alan Coxon • Jim Cowie • Stef
Chris Galvin • Kevin Cape • Jeff Galvin • Regis Negrier • A
Terry Tinton • Derek Quelch • Mark Dodson • Paul Gayler
Allan Picket • Neil Thrift • Peter Fiori • Philip Corrick • Stephe
David Simms • Rob Kirby • Herbert Berger • John W
Tony Cameron • Daniel Richardson • Jason Atherton • Yolan
Richard Tonks • Martyn Nail • Peter A. Jones • Alain
Sara Jane Stanes • Alan Coxon • Jim Cowie • Stef
Chris Galvin • Kevin Cape • Jeff Galvin • Regis Negrier • A
Terry Tinton • Derek Quelch • Mark Dodson • Paul Gayler
Allan Picket • Neil Thrift • Peter Fiori • Philip Corrick • Stephe
David Simms • Rob Kirby • Herbert Berger • John W
Tony Cameron • Daniel Richardson • Jason Atherton • Yolan
Richard Tonks • Martyn Nail • Peter A. Jones • Alain
Sara Jane Stanes • Alan Coxon • Jim Cowie • Stef
Chris Galvin • Kevin Cape • Jeff Galvin • Regis Negrier • A